## Praise for *Pure Love*

"The author takes readers on an unexpected journey of enlightenment as he probes the depths of his soul to ultimately transform profound grief into healing and higher understanding. *Pure Love* is pure joy — indescribable beauty in its purest form."

CRAIG LEENER,
Author of *There's No Basketball on Mars*

"This inspirational work derives its beauty from the searing honesty expressed by grieving parents over the death of their only daughter at the age of 35, and from the depth of the conversations her father has had with her ever since. The conversations offer a validation of what many experience: ongoing communication from "across the veil." The messages themselves are stunning in their hope, positivity, and depth. A book to keep nearby."

MARIANNE HERR-PAUL, D.O.
Greencastle, PA

"As a physician for over 45 years, I cared for thousands of patients. One of the worst life experiences any of my patients ever told me about was losing a child, especially when that child had become an adult. John Mears and his wife Mamie lost their daughter Angela in her thirties. Soon after Angela passed, John began to experience Angela whispering messages of comfort, hope and purpose during his daily meditations. These communications have helped him make sense of this seemingly senseless tragedy, and they form the basis for most of this book. It contains universal elements that anyone can apply positively to their own life. I heartily recommend this book, especially to those experiencing a personal loss similar to John and Mamie's."

DR. J. MICHAEL HERR,
Retired

# PURE LOVE

# PURE LOVE

## Our Daughter's First Whispers After Death

John Mears

**LITTLE
DRAGON**
PRESS

Copyright © 2024 by John Mears

All rights reserved.

Printed in the United States of America. No part of this book may be reproduced in any manner whatsoever without written permission except in the case of brief quotations embodied in critical articles and reviews.

For more information, visit www.Angelasbook.com.

Interior text design by Backstory Design

PB ISBN: 979-8-9916611-0-2
EBOOK ISBN: 979-8-9916611-1-9

10 9 8 7 6 5 4 3 2 1

Dedication

To our parents, who were the first to teach us about
pure, unselfish love by their example.

# Contents

# Foreword

My name is Marjan Bakhtiyari. I am a licensed clinical psychologist in the Los Angeles area. This book is of special interest to me because of its relevance to my work.

Grief is a universal yet deeply personal journey, a complex emotional landscape that we navigate in the wake of profound loss. As a therapist, in grief therapy, I have walked alongside many clients who have lost adult children. Each story is unique, yet the pain is a common thread that binds them. The loss of a child, regardless of age, disrupts the natural order of life and challenges every aspect of our being — emotionally, psychologically, and spiritually.

*Pure Love: Our Daughter's First Whispers After Death* is more than a memoir; it is a testament to the enduring power of love and the human spirit's capacity for healing. In this poignant narrative, John and his wife share the intimate journey of their daughter Angela's presence beyond her physical departure. Their words resonate deeply with the experiences of many who have faced similar losses, offering a blend of vulnerability, wisdom, and hope.

As a psychologist, I am profoundly moved by the way this book integrates the psychological aspects of grief with a spiritual dimension. It beautifully captures the essence of resilience and post-traumatic growth — concepts that are vital in the grieving process. Through meditation and a focus on enduring bonds, John guides readers toward finding purpose and meaning after loss.

The messages from Angela, filled with love and light, echo the therapeutic principles that I encourage in my practice. They serve as gentle reminders that our connections to our loved ones transcend the physical world. The book emphasizes secure attachment and enduring bonds, which are not only comforting but also foundational for psychological healing.

In my experience working with clients who have lost adult children, the themes presented in this book — of infinite meaning, secure attachment, and the transformative power of love — are invaluable. They offer solace to those navigating the darkest corridors of grief, illustrating that while the pain of loss never fully dissipates, it is possible to find peace, purpose, and even joy again.

*Pure Love* stands as a beacon of light, guiding those in mourning toward a renewed sense of hope and connection. It is a powerful reminder that even in our most challenging moments, love has the capacity to heal, transform, and enlighten.

I am honored to contribute this foreword, and I hope that readers will find the same sense of comfort and inspiration that I have discovered in these pages.

Dr. Marjan Bakhtiyari, Psy.D.

Introductions
by
John and Mamie Mears

## John's Side of This

Around the world, at least two people die every second. On March 27th, 2023, our only child, Angela Ingrid Mears, became one of those people at the age of thirty-five.

My wife Mamie and I have each had very different experiences of grief, but together we have been able to move forward. Creating this book is part of how we have survived.

The first part of this book is about how we experienced our first three months after Angela died. Future books in this series will deal with our continuing journey.

We use the words "died" and "death" reluctantly.

First, neither of us wants to believe that our daughter is gone forever.

Second, we have experienced numerous weird occurrences that suggest our daughter might still be around in some form or other. We will detail some of that weird stuff in this and future books.

Third, on the day after the health emergency leading to our daughter's death, I started to feel Angela's presence. For some, that will sound weird. For many others who have had similar experiences, that might offer a measure of comfort.

In *Treasure Island* by Robert Louis Stevenson, Long John Silver says, "Them's that die'll be the lucky ones." After Angela died, my wife Mamie has often said her life is so painful that she no longer wants to live. However, our lifelong partnership has helped both of us continue in this world without our daughter. Here we offer ideas from our tool kit for surviving grief as a couple.

Firstly, we have agreed upon the following:

- Kindness towards one another.
- Respect for one another.
- Patience with one another.
- Doing as many things together as possible.
- Accepting the comfort of friends and family.
- Giving each other the space and permission to process grief in our own way.

Secondly, we have been greatly helped by creative outlets: for me writing, music, photography, and gardening; for Mamie, cooking and writing text messages in a one-sided conversation with Angela.

Thirdly, I have found some measure of hope and healing in therapy, exercise, yoga, and meditation. I have also found a harmless outlet for my rage and frustration by playing violent computer games.

Fourth, I have discovered something many people have grown up with: Faith. I discovered this belatedly because of a feeling that our daughter was and is still with us. This gives me faith in the universe. Angela's gentle wisdom and inspiration have been for me a source of healing and a river of comfort and blessings, far beyond anything I can describe or share with words. Angela's inspiration has given me renewed faith in myself.

We hope that what we are sharing here will be of some help and comfort to you, dear reader.


## Mamie's Side of This

I am not a writer, so I am writing this with the help of my husband John. I immigrated from China in 1980. English is my second language. In fact, John was my English teacher.

John says he can feel Angela, and almost hear her whispering to him. He tells me those things give him comfort. Nothing gives me comfort. John is a loving husband, and together we have been able to survive. But Angela's death has caused a gaping hole where my hopes and dreams once were.

I was born in China after Mao Zedong's Communist Party took control in 1949. I grew up in many kinds of craziness and hell, including the famine from 1958 to 1962, when we always felt hungry; my father's arrest and five and a half years in prison, as a suspected spy for the West; and Mao's "Cultural Revolution," when gangs of youths called "Red Guards" were given police powers and allowed to loot private homes and attack whoever they wanted. In 2012, I almost died in the operating room due to blood loss during open-heart surgery. For at least six months afterward, I was very weak and depressed, and could not walk up more than three steps at a time.

But if you put together all the suffering in my life before March 27, 2023, it was not nearly as bad as the emotional and physical pain of the year since Angela died.

I worked hard my whole life, building a nice family in the USA with John. But losing Angela was the hardest thing I have ever had to deal with. I still can't believe that she is really gone from this world. I don't think I can ever recover from this.

No one can truly understand the impact that dreadful morning has had on my life. My heart has been ripped out again. My life has been totally shattered. I feel detached from everything and everyone. I will never be the same. There is this big, deep hole, a crater in my heart and it will never be filled again. I just want my life to be over soon.

I feel lost, angry, empty, and alone. Suffocated. My heart is in constant pain. I really don't want to live like this. I am kind of dead inside already. I feel detached from everything. I don't know where or how to go on.

Every day seems worse than the day before, and I wake up every morning dreading every minute of this life, which has become for me a kind of torture. I wonder what terrible things I did in past lives to deserve this.

Every day I want to die, and many times a day I am troubled by fantasies of killing myself. But I continue, because I am surrounded by so much love, by people who need me and want me to stick around.

John has stood by me through my worst days, but some days I hate everything in this world.

Old friends of mine have been wonderful. Their phone calls and visits have helped. I also feel comfort when friends of Angela's reach out. Angela touched so many lives, helped and inspired so many people, including us.

Maybe this book will help and inspire others who have to go through this unbearable experience of losing a child, especially an adult child, and — worst of all — an only child.

Since Angela died, I have been writing messages to her. This has been a kind of therapy for me. I will share one text to Angela: "I love you with all my heart 🤍 with pure, unconditional love to you forever."

# Prologue

Before March 27, 2023, Mamie and I had what could reasonably be called "the perfect life" in Southern California. After decades of working hard, saving money, raising our daughter, and surviving earthquakes, wildfires, recessions, gang violence, burglaries and riots, we had both retired and were enjoying our golden years. Our house was paid for. I was teaching English to immigrants part-time, work that I dearly love. Energetic gardening and ample rains had turned our backyard into a visual paradise, with blooming fuchsia ice plants and bright-green St. Augustine grass.

Mamie and I would sit at our breakfast table, look at each other and say, "How did we get so lucky?"

The icing on the cake for us was Angela, our amazing, blazing daughter. Straight out of college, Angela was recruited into Weber Shandwick, which on its web page calls itself "one of the world's leading global public relations firms with offices in major media, business and government capitals around the world." Weber is part of the Interpublic Group of Companies, Inc. (IPG), the fourth largest advertising company in the USA.

At Weber, Angela started as an intern at Weber's Chicago offices. She rocketed up through the ranks, leading creative work for the agency on the West Coast and in Chicago, Europe and New York. She worked with clients such as Airbnb, McDonald's, Ikea, Unilever, Haleon, IBM, AB InBev, VMware and Sony. Her work was recognized by PR/advertising organizations including Cannes Lions, Eurobest, Clios, the One Show, the Webby's, the Shorty awards, and the PRWeek Awards. She was named to Campaign's 2022 Female Frontier Awards list. However, we knew very little about any of this until after she died. She chose not to be her own PR client with friends and family.

In June 2022, Angela was named Weber's global executive creative director and in September of the same year she stepped into one of the most enviable positions in her PR/marketing profession: Chief Creative Officer at Weber's New York office.

*Angela, third from the right, with colleagues in Buenos Aires, Argentina March 2023*

Angela turned thirty-five on February 26, 2023. She had already moved to New York City, where she was busy getting settled into a one-bedroom apartment with a view of the Empire State Building.

On March 22, Angela flew to Buenos Aires, Argentina, to serve on a jury that would choose winning entries in an annual competition among advertising companies from around the world. She was wowing global industry leaders when it happened.

Trigger warning: Part One of this book is very sad. If you want to skip to the more hopeful and inspiring sections — Part Two, etc. — have at it. Because God knows we all need more hope and less sadness. I know I do.

# Angela's Body

# CHAPTER 1

# The Hours and Days after It Happened

On March 27th, 2023, at around 7:30 AM, Mamie's cell phone rang and woke us up. This was strange, because the phone had been set to "Do not disturb." Half asleep, we let it ring, but Mamie saw that the call was from Angela's husband Charlie, whom we had designated as an exception to the "Do not disturb" setting. I was annoyed at Charlie. "Kind of inconsiderate, calling at this hour."

We tried to go back to sleep, but Mamie thought, "What if Charlie's calling about Angela?" She disabled the "Do not disturb" control. On her phone, she now saw half a dozen voice and text messages that had started coming in after 6:20 AM Pacific Daylight Time.

She called Charlie back, but he didn't answer.

Then she started reading the text messages.

The first was a WhatsApp missed call, followed by a text at

6:22 AM, from a number we didn't recognize: "Angela is having an emergency. Can you please call me ASAP?"

The second was a text from an "Ariel" at 6:23 AM. "Angela is having an emergency here in Buenos Aires. She is OK right now but going to the hospital. Please call me. Ariel with the judging program."

The third text was a WhatsApp at 6:24 from an unrecognized number: "Hello, is this the emergency contact of Angela?"

The fourth was at 6:29 AM: "Hi, Your daughter, Angela Mears, has had a medical emergency while working in Buenos Aires, Argentina. Please call us back as soon as you can. We have left you a voice mail." That text was from Gina Grillo, CEO and President of the Advertising Club of New York, and head of ANDY, the organization sponsoring the annual advertising competition.

There were also two voice messages from a "Sarah" at 6:27 AM. The first said that Angela was having a health "episode" in Buenos Aires. The second, at 6:49 AM (also from Sarah), said that they had arrived at the hospital, and that they needed more medical information.

Mamie called Sarah back.

Sarah said Angela had fainted and was in a coma, but was stable in a hospital. She added that Mamie should fly to Buenos Aires as soon as possible.

Then Charlie returned our call. His voice was breaking. He told Mamie that Angela had had a stroke in Buenos Aires. "Her brain has shut down," he managed between sobs. He was saying that doctors in the USA and Argentina were trying to see what could be done, but that it didn't look at all hopeful. Charlie had been getting detailed medical information from doctors in Vigilant Medical, a consultancy group working for Weber Shandwick.

Mamie and I bought the first available ticket for Mamie to fly to Buenos Aires. The ticket was one-way, since there were so many unknowns: Would Angela recover from her coma? How long could that take? If she did recover, how completely? Would she need rehabilitation?

Or was it even worse than we could imagine?

Since this was an international flight, we had to take photos of Mamie's passport and upload those to the United Airlines website. Our hands kept shaking. It took forever.

We packed Mamie's bags quickly, with enough of her heart medication for ten days. I drove her to LAX for a 1:00 PM flight to Buenos Aires, via Houston. I would stay in L.A. to take care of the house, pay the bills, and handle communications and whatever else came up.

Mamie suffers from sciatica and had a physical therapy appointment that afternoon. We canceled that appointment.

♡♡

Feeling somewhat lost and alone, I started sharing the news on Facebook at 2:14 PM:

> Dear friends and family,
> This morning my wife and I received some troubling news. Our daughter Angela, who is in Buenos Aires,

Argentina on business, suffered a very bad stroke and is in grave condition. Her prognosis is uncertain at this time. Apparently, it looks pretty bad. She is in a coma.

Whether or not you believe in prayer, meditation, God, Buddha, Jesus, angels or whatever, please send Angela all the best spiritual energy you can.

The response was overwhelming. On Facebook I have for years posted photos, poems, memes, and political commentary with monotonous frequency, but rarely get more than half a dozen "Likes" or comments. Within hours, my post about Angela got more than 200 "Likes" and comments, expressing shock and support. Cousins, nieces, and nephews sent their love. Friends from work sent their love. Former students sent their love. Even people from whom I had not heard a peep in a decade sent their love.

As it turns out, there's a lot of love in this world.

Especially when it's most desperately needed.

I called my little sister Margie with the news. She said "Oh, John," and started sobbing uncontrollably. So did I. It helped.

Margie called my little brother Bill, from whom I had been estranged for years. He called me, offering to visit. His son Max had died the year before, so he could empathize.

I made a few more phone calls, including one to the school where I work to let them know I would be absent.

On Facebook, messages of sympathy and support kept pouring in. Jennifer Alison Poole, Angela's high school English teacher (now Vice Principal and English teacher at Chaminade

College Preparatory, in Woodland Hills), organized a prayer group.

A retired teacher with whom I'd ceased communication because of personal differences called me in tears. So did my older sister Nancy and my niece Jordan and my brother's ex-wife Odette. I felt surrounded by warmth and loving kindness.

I would need it.

My wife would need it even more.

I want to interject here a strange occurrence. On March 27th, 2023 — within minutes of Angela's health emergency in Buenos Aires — Angela's dog Bernie threw up. He vomited. Bernie is a young, very healthy dog who never throws up.

Bernie was with Angela's husband Charlie, who was in Nashville, Tennessee, on business, at the time. Charlie was puzzled. Had Bernie eaten something he shouldn't have?

Soon after Bernie vomited, Charlie got a call from Angela's company, Weber Shandwick. A Weber representative told Charlie that Angela had collapsed and was in the hospital, stable. The Weber representative put Charlie in touch with Vigilant Medical, the group of U.S. doctors hired by Weber Shandwick to give expert medical opinions. The Vigilant doctors were already in touch with doctors at the hospital in Buenos Aires, and gave Charlie updates and details, which were all quite upsetting.

But Bernie throwing up? That was weird.

It was just the start of weirdness, what I like to call "anomalous occurrences." More of those to come.

♡♡

Mamie's flight to Buenos Aires was the worst flight of her life. She had made many international, longer flights before, between the USA and China and Europe. But this was different.

Was Angela alive or dead? Would she live or die? Was she brain-dead? Would she be a vegetable for the rest of her life?

After a stopover in Houston, Mamie's plane landed in Buenos Aires at approximately 8 AM (Argentina Time or ART) on March 28th. It took an hour for her to get through customs. Standing in line was agony because of her sciatica.

She was met outside the airport by four people in a mini-van: a driver holding up her name; Guillermo Garcia (Weber representative in Buenos Aires); Sarah Cadenhead (ANDY juror); and Gina Grillo (CEO and President of the Advertising Club of New York). As they drove to the hospital, Sarah and Gina told Mamie that Angela was in a coma, and that someone was with her to make sure she was okay.

They drove straight to the hospital, arriving around 10 AM ART.

The Hospital General de Agudos Dr. Argerich is one of several public hospitals in Buenos Aires. It is a beige brick building with eight floors. They arrived at the emergency entrance on the side of the building and were directed down several narrow hallways to "el shock room" — what people in the USA call the emergency room.

Mamie was met in the hospital hallway by Angela's doctor, a tall, middle-aged man wearing a mask. He talked to Mamie in broken English, saying Angela was basically brain dead, and that they were keeping her on life support so that they could harvest her organs.

Mamie went numb. How could this be happening?

She asked to go in and see Angela in "el shock room."

The room had six beds, all occupied by patients. Angela was intubated and hooked to an artificial ventilator. Mamie tried opening Angela's eyelids. The pupils were dilated and un-responsive. Mamie knew at that point that Angela was gone.

Nurses hurried Mamie out of the shock room because they had to help other patients. She went to the hallway, which had no chairs or benches. Exhausted and aching from sciatica, she sat on the floor and tried calling me, but I was fast asleep, it being around 6 AM PDT. She left message after message, begging me to answer the phone or call her back. I finally heard the phone ringing and woke up, too late to catch the call. I called her back. Mamie was furious. "Why didn't you pick up the phone?"

"I'm so sorry, honey. I was sleeping."

Sobbing, she told me the doctors didn't think Angela could be saved. "Should we take her to another hospital? Should we find other doctors?"

I said, "Honey, we might just need to face reality."

She sobbed, "You sound so cold!"

I felt like the worst person in the world. But growing up with two MD parents, one of them a surgeon, I had often taken phone messages about Dad's patients in the hospital who had "expired." Accordingly, I had developed a certain emotional distance about death.

But this was our daughter.

This was different.

There was nothing more for Mamie to do at the hospital, so she went to the hotel. Weber and the ANDY organization were paying for Mamie to stay in the Faena hotel, where the ANDYs jury was meeting. It's a posh establishment with red velvet and gold trimmings everywhere.

Room service brought a Caesar salad, ordered by Sarah. Mamie hadn't eaten for more than twenty-four hours, but she could only swallow a bite. She had no appetite, and her throat didn't seem to be working.

Nothing was real.

At 1:00 PM, Mamie joined a conference call with Sarah and a Dr. Gossman from the Vigilant group. Dr. Gossman said they had received all the relevant information from the hospital, and it appeared that the hospital staff had done everything correctly.

One slightly hopeful sign emerged. At the hospital, doctors noticed a small glimmer of brain activity. Mamie asked if this meant that there was hope. Dr. Gossman said only time would tell. The next 24-48 hours would be critical.

Mamie called me with this information, which I passed on to Facebook with the comment: "Continued thoughts and prayers might be the ticket. Miracles can and do happen. Every one of us is a miracle of survival at every moment."

After I posted the above, I was meditating when I felt a quiet whisper:

*I'm so sorry, Daddy. I didn't understand you. Now I do. You were right all along. The physical is temporary. The spiritual is permanent. Not the other way around. Now meditate. Be with me.*

I meditated some more, and felt more of what I desperately wanted to believe was Angela's voice.

*Daddy, this was meant to be. I will help you with your writing. It is important for the world.*
*Tell Mommy I want to be free. Let me go.*

I thought: Disconnect the ventilator?

*Yes, but not yet.*

Then another whisper:

*Those with little spiritual awareness cling to the physical as the only reality, but they are sadly mistaken.*

Meanwhile, in Buenos Aires, after the conference call, the hotel staff finally took Mamie to Angela's room, 609. There was a red tassel on the doorknob. Gina explained that it meant "DO

NOT DISTURB." The room had not been opened since Angela left it on March 27th.

The bell person opened the door for them. When Mamie went in and saw all Angela's belongings, she had to sit down and sob.

Mamie composed herself and went back to the hospital with Pilar (a translator hired by IPG) and Ceci (an IPG employee). The bedsheets on Angela's hospital bed were stained with blood. Mamie complained. Why hadn't the hospital changed the sheets? A nurse yelled at Mamie in Spanish and rushed her out of the shock room. Mamie called Gina and said she wanted to transfer Angela to another hospital. Gina started working on it.

Mamie stayed at the hospital with Ceci, Guillermo, and Pilar. Whenever she was permitted in the shock room, which was only for perhaps five minutes at a time, Mamie stood next to Angela, whispering in her ear and holding her hand.

Early that evening, Ceci drove Mamie and Pilar back to the hotel. Mamie ordered room service spaghetti, but could only eat a couple bites.

Two of Angela's closest and dearest friends arrived from the USA to help Mamie through this ordeal: Mananya Komorowski, a coworker at Weber Shandwick; and Angela's husband Charlie Witkowski. Charlie and Mananya got to the hotel at approximately 8:30 PM ART. Another IPG employee named Jorge drove them all to the hospital. After they waited around forty-five minutes, the on-duty doctor came and said they were keeping a close watch on Angela to monitor her brain activity. She was still intubated and completely unresponsive.

Mamie, Charlie, and Mananya gathered around Angela and whispered into her ear. Mamie held Angela's hand and her feet. Mananya played messages from friends at Weber into her ear. Angela was completely unresponsive. However, Mamie still clung to the faint hope that Angela might show some sign of recovery.

There was none. They went back to the hotel and tried to sleep.

## March 29, 2023

After 9 AM ART, Gina brought news to Mamie and the others: private hospital doctors would be coming soon to review the case.

At around 10 AM ART, Mamie, Charlie, Mananya, and Guillermo went back to the hospital. They were greeted by the director of the hospital and shown to a private room. Did they want anything? Water? They each got a plastic bottle of water.

The hospital's female head of neurosurgery and a male psychiatrist came in. They had continued doing tests, which now showed no sign of brain activity. Angela was essentially brain dead, and the damage was irreversible.

The psychiatrist asked if they had considered organ donation. Mamie said she had to think about it.

Two top doctors from local private hospitals came and

talked to the hospital staff. They looked at Angela's test results, reviewing everything. There was another meeting in the private room with the private hospital doctors. The doctors agreed that Angela was brain dead, and the damage was irreversible.

At approximately 9:20 AM PDT, I got a call from Buenos Aires, where it was already 1:20 PM.

Mananya was talking in a dry, official capacity. She told me that Angela was now showing no brain activity. Doctors both in Buenos Aires and in the USA, after looking at all CT scans and other medical information, had reached consensus that Angela was brain dead, and that, with the consent of the family, her organs should be harvested as soon as possible. Angela had specified on her driver's license that she wanted to be an organ donor.

Mananya asked me what I wanted to happen with Angela's body. I said I felt her wishes for organ donation should be honored, and that cremation made the most sense.

Mananya then told Mamie what I'd said. Mamie said, "That's what he wants. I don't have to agree."

Mamie, Charlie, and Mananya went outside the front entrance of the hospital with the entourage from IPG, including Pilar. After some thought, and after looking at Angela's driver's license, Mamie decided to honor Angela's wishes for organ donation. Charlie agreed to cremation, because Angela had told him that she did not want to be buried, but to be cremated and have her ashes spread around in different places.

Mananya told me to meditate, which I did. Again, it felt as though Angela was whispering to my heart:

*Daddy, we have important work to do. This is our destiny. This is what we were always meant to do. This work is what you and I were born to do. We will now be writing partners.*

I sadly whispered in my heart: "We will no longer see your happy smile."

*We all must now be a happy smile.*
*You will find peace in this madness.*
*People are afraid of the abyss, but this is infinite light and joy and peace.*
*Daddy. This world is completely different. It's like this world, the spiritual world, is right side up, and the physical world is the upside down. But they have to be more together, Daddy. We have to be the bridge between worlds. We will bring the two worlds more together, more in harmony. But that can only happen by bringing the spiritual into the physical. The spiritual must dominate. This will bring heaven on Earth.*

"Heaven on Earth" is a phrase used by Maharishi Mahesh Yogi in predicting how the world could be when enough people meditate. Having practiced Maharishi's Transcendental Meditation (TM) for more than fifty-one years, I wondered if I was projecting my TM mentality into my inner dialogue with Angela. I wondered if I was making up this whole inner conversation with Angela as a kind of psychotic delusion to help me cope with the devastation of losing our only child.

My mother, Virginia Mears MD, was a psychiatrist. Once I told her about an acquaintance who claimed to be hearing voices. According to those voices, I was supposed to lead an exodus from Planet Earth to the moons of Saturn. Mom told me that in psychoses where people hear voices, the brain seems to manufacture a kind of Greek chorus to validate whatever the person wants to hear. I wondered if that was happening to me.

I still do.

However, a growing number of what Carl Jung might have called "synchronicities," or what I will call "anomalous occurrences," lend credibility to the mystical and perhaps unbelievable idea that our daughter was and still is communicating with me from beyond the grave. Angela's dog Bernie threw up within minutes of her death, more than 5,200 miles away. That was just the first of many anomalous occurrences that I will detail in the following chapters and in future books.

Around midnight on March 29th, Mamie, Charlie, and Mananya saw Angela's body being wheeled into the elevator for organ donation.

They went back to the hotel. Numb, they showered and went to bed.

# CHAPTER 2

# The Days after Angela Was Declared Dead

In the early hours of Thursday, March 30th, a team of Argentine doctors harvested Angela's organs and took them out of the room in refrigerated boxes.  Mamie, Charlie, and Mananya now had to identify Angela's body prior to cremation.

Back in Los Angeles, I was sleepless and depressed, but I had the far easier job of taking care of the house and paying the bills. Resting in my favorite easy chair, I felt Angela — or perhaps my imagination — whispering these words of comfort:

*Daddy, rest, but don't give up.*
*I'm with you and Mommy and anybody, anytime you want*
*or need.*

*Everything is completely different here. Physical distance has no meaning. Physical boundaries have no meaning.*

*However, human life in the physical world is tremendously meaningful. One could even say it's infinitely meaningful because human beings have the ability to experience and join with the pure love, brilliant intelligence, and unlimited creative power at the heart of the universe, also known as God. They can also work closely with God in many important, exciting, and amazing ways. This is a unique feature of the human being that is the envy of sentient things, both physical and non-physical or spiritual, throughout the universe.*

*Daddy, we can write together. I can be your new Gerry*, only on a purely spiritual level.*


I also received a flood of emails and text messages from people who knew Angela (see Appendix).

In Buenos Aires, at around 10:30 AM ART, Mamie and Charlie, accompanied by the IPG entourage, went to the hospital for Angela's death certificate. The paperwork was complicated by the fact that Angela was a foreign citizen, plus the documentation was in Spanish. Guillermo translated and Charlie

---

*Gerry Keston, an elderly British gentleman from the East End of London (retired from the Royal Air Force intelligence service), was my writing partner — and a frequent visitor to our house — for more than twenty years. Angela grew up with Gerry standing in as a kind of adoptive grandfather.

signed. Charlie also communicated with the U.S. embassy in Buenos Aires and got their referral for a funeral home.

On Friday, March 31st, Mamie went with Charlie, Mananya, and Guillermo to the morgue in the hospital basement to officially identify Angela's body. The funeral director met them in the basement hallway.  The morgue had a thick steel door resembling that of a frozen meat locker, with a strong, thick handle. Inside, it was very cold. There was a twenty-foot corridor, at the end of which there were drawers in the wall where bodies were stored. Angela's corpse had been placed in a temporary casket on the floor.

It was her body. Her skin and lips were pale. Mamie touched her face. It was cold. Mamie kissed her daughter's body on the forehead for the last time.

That final moment has haunted my wife ever since.

The funeral director drove them back to the hotel. Charlie filled out more forms at the hotel. Now they had to wait for the cremains, which wouldn't be available for five days.

Back in Los Angeles, I felt a weight on my soul, heavier than I had ever felt in my life. Meditation gave me some relief, but our only daughter — our amazing, blazing girl — was gone.

But again, in meditation, I felt this whisper:

*Daddy, I'm not gone. I just changed form. I'm free now. I escaped that prison cell and can now go anywhere and be with anyone.*

*Be gentle and patient. Take care of yourself and Mommy. Everything and everyone else can wait.*

On April 2nd, we received news that, by donating her organs, Angela had saved two lives in Argentina. Her right kidney and liver had saved a fifty-year-old female on March 31st. Angela's left kidney and pancreas had saved another female, twenty-six. Both of Angela's corneas were being distributed.

For Mamie and me, this news brought a shred of gladness and peace of mind. Meanwhile, Angela's company, Weber Shandwick, and the ANDY Awards organization were going the extra mile — in fact, many extra miles — with kindness and generosity. Together, they paid for all travel expenses incurred by Mamie, Charlie, and Mananya, including airfare, food, and lodging. They had also hired pricey medical specialists, in both the USA and Argentina, for their professional opinions.

Mamie was suffering from sciatica in Buenos Aires and had no idea how to get help with physical therapy (PT). By Facebook text message, I contacted Susan Howe, the Weber executive who had recruited Angela into the company. Susan was now President of Weber Shandwick. Susan responded:

> John, I'm so sorry for your loss. Truly Angela touched me and so many of us at Weber with her light and spirit. In the gatherings we've had we've all decided we want to "be like Angela." Develop people. And ideas. Always dance. Take the stage.
>
> I reached out to Mananya re PT… As usual, Mananya was on it.

Also on April 2, Mamie received the following text message

on her cell phone from Tiffany Rolfe, Global Chief Creative Officer at R/GA, a global marketing company affiliated with IPG. R/GA clients include Nike, Verizon, Samsung, Airbnb, Slack, ESPN, and Instagram. Ms. Rolfe leads a team of over two hundred creatives. With her permission, I am sharing her entire message because it offers a vivid firsthand account of Angela's final moments.

Forgive my long note but I wanted to reach out and express my condolences on losing your beautiful and talented Angela.

I was with Angela in Buenos Aires. I was the head of the ANDYs jury and I'm also CCO* like Angela was. You have met my coworker Josefina who is the Exec Creative Director of our Argentina office. I wanted to share what my experience was with her before and during the trip. I'm not sure if it helps you at all but maybe knowing a little of her last days gives you something extra. And other jurors want to share their memories of her as well, so I'll collect those — and we've been collecting the video and images of those days. Josefina will share with you at dinner next week.

As background, I'm one of the few female CCOs out there (there aren't a ton of us), just like Angela is, and I'd met her at the IPG leadership lab a few months ago where

---

*By way of explanation, CCO = Chief Creative Officer. This is the highest position possible on the creative side of the marketing industry. Angela had been promoted to that position at Weber Shandwick's international headquarters in New York City.

we were both chosen to attend — our agencies have the same holding company (IPG). We connected instantly. She'd shared with me that she was a fan of my agency and had been to many of my talks in Cannes, which was very flattering. I could tell right away she was a force. I was looking forward to getting to know her better and watch her take over the industry, especially when I found out she was moving to NY. She expressed interest on getting more visibility and I'd mentioned I would love to try and help get her involved in more industry events and juries.

When I had the opportunity to invite people onto the jury I was leading, she was first on my list. I knew she'd bring a fresh new perspective. And she did. She stood out right away among the group with her wit and strength in her opinions. We also all shared some personal stories, so we got to know each other over just a few days.

Then, Monday morning, as we were beginning the first day of deliberations on what should win the award show, she came in and was one of the first to talk about the work she wanted to fight for. She even walked across the room to catch up with some other jurors and was laughing and having a great time. She was so sharp, never could I have imagined what happened minutes later. She just stood up and collapsed. We all thought she'd fainted.

As the head of the jury, and as a woman who has fainted in front of others before, I immediately wanted her to feel comforted and not feel embarrassment. I had fainted at a work event before and it was very embarrassing to me. So while we attended her we asked the jury to take a break.

And we immediately had the hotel call 911 — but minutes in, we knew this wasn't a normal faint. I was at her side, along with the ANDYs team and a couple of other jurors — Josefina included, who is Argentinian, to ensure that we were communicating clearly in Spanish to the hotel and to the ER.

Those mins felt like an eternity, but we held her arms and ensured she knew we were there. We tried to make her comfortable, laid her down on pillows, caressed her face, held her hands and talked to her so she didn't feel alone or scared. She couldn't really speak, but I could tell she was there through her eyes. But her condition worsened so quickly…

The ER came and knew it was neurological immediately. So as she went to the ER, we all connected to important locals who knew of the best neuro-physicians in BA and the doctors at the hospital she was at, to ensure we were doing everything we could to give her the best care possible. I have children, one is a daughter, and I kept thinking about you all and knowing that I'd want to look you in the eyes and tell you we did everything we could to help her, to save her and her brilliance and bright spirit. Just as I'd want others to do for my own daughter in this situation.

I know that hearing this can't really help much, but I do want you to know that she was in her element those 4 days, expressing her creativity and knowledge and passion for the work she does, and meeting and impressing new friends with her wit, her talent, her knowledge of food…

I want to do whatever I can to help her spirit continue. I'm here to help you all do something to honor her and help her continue to make the impact I knew she would have made in this world, for so many people. I'm here if you need anything.

—Tiff

As the child of two politically liberal parents, and as a teacher working under a union contract at a large public school district (LAUSD), I will confess to having a default anti-corporate mentality. However, the more I was exposed to the people Angela worked with in the advertising and marketing business — people like Tiffany Rolfe, Gina Grillo, Susan Howe — and others, the more I saw humanity, warm-heartedness and magnanimity. For me, this is a big deal. It says to me that, after all, there is hope for our nation and the world.

On Tuesday April 4th, at 11 AM ART, Mamie and Charlie went to the U.S. embassy in Buenos Aires to deal with bureaucratic details concerning the death of our daughter. As they were finding out, the paperwork gets complicated when a U.S. citizen dies in a foreign country.

At the embassy door, they had to check all their belongings, for which they got a claim check with the number "88."

I'd like to spend a moment on the number "8," because that number has shown up often in our lives.

In Chinese culture, "8" is the luckiest number, because it

means wealth and/or good fortune. The number "8" has appeared over and over again for Mamie and me in our marriage and parenting. We met on January 26th (2 + 6 = 8). We were married on July 26th (again, 2 + 6 = 8). Our first apartment was 1917 17th Street, Santa Monica (1 + 7 = 8). Angela was born on February 26, 1988. In addition to the "26" and the double 8s in the number itself, the year "1988" adds up to 8 (1 + 9 + 8 + 8 = 26, 2 + 6 = 8).

Additionally, when you add up all the numbers of the dates in Mamie's birthday you get the number "5." When you add mine, you get the number "3." These two numbers are called "destiny numbers" in numerology. Adding Mamie's destiny number and mine, you get "8."

The number 8 also appeared freakishly often when Charlie, Mamie, and Mananya were in Buenos Aires. They passed billboards plastered with the number 8. The fare for the first Uber Charlie Witkowski took after Angela passed away was 888 pesos. And of course at the embassy, where they had to turn in all their belongings, their claim ticket was 88.

Watch for more "anomalous occurrences"    including more on the number 8 — as you read on.

♡♡

Meanwhile, in Los Angeles, we got a flood of flowers for Angela. In our mailbox, in my email, and on Facebook, condolences and praise for our daughter came nonstop. On April 4th, I received this on Facebook Messenger text from Andy Polansky, retired CEO of Weber Shandwick:

John, I worked closely with your daughter during her time at Weber Shandwick and wanted to reach out to you and your wife to offer my deepest condolences. I was CEO at Weber for many years and I can say without hesitation that Angela was one of our brightest lights. She and I traveled together to Detroit several times for important meetings with our largest agency client, General Motors. While it was terrific to see Angela and her considerable brainpower and creative prowess in action, it was our side conversations about life and cooking and all kinds of things that I remember most. A visit to Chicago and a catch-up with Angela was my first business trip during the pandemic, after having stopped traveling for months.

I am sorry to send this note via Facebook but don't have your home address.

May Angela's memory be a blessing to you and your wife. As I'm sure you have heard from others at Weber we will miss her tremendously.

Sincerely,

Andy Polansky

Another corporate big-wig. Another spontaneous act of kindness.

Angela had lifted hearts and touched lives deeply around the world, and at many levels of the corporate world. More than we had ever imagined possible.

On Thursday, April 6th, Mamie, Charlie, and Mananya boarded a flight back to L.A. with Angela's ashes in a wooden box. During that trip, Mamie got a text message from Gina Grillo saying that, because of Angela's death, they were changing the date for the ANDYs awards ceremony in New York City from April 20th to May 10th. We were all invited to that ceremony.

In the San Fernando Valley, I was resting in bed when the following came to me:

*There is a vast spiritual network of healing and connectivity, of which I am now a part. It is my joy to extend that to you and Mommy. You are never alone. This is your destiny, Daddy, to help bring spiritual consciousness to the human race. It is urgently vital at this time especially.*

*Daddy, this was meant to be. It was the plan all along. Teach the world.*

*I'm now free in blessed realms of joy. From this side, drugs seem pointless. They are like smashing a car window to get in. Meditation is like using the key.*

*Daddy, pure love is a great theme. Let's run with it.*

*Pure love and being loving have become clichés, but regardless, they are by far the most important things about human life. Many people seem to feel that love and being loving make them more vulnerable and put them in danger, but in fact, pure love is the most powerful protection a person can have. And pure love is the safest thing there is. No actions motivated by loving kindness are ever wasted, even if those for whom the love is felt or shown do not appreciate or reciprocate.*

*Daddy, a bright road stretches ahead of us.*

On the morning of April 7th, Mamie, Charlie, and Mananya arrived with Angela's ashes at LAX, where they were greeted by close family, myself included. They had been traveling more than fifteen hours and were exhausted. We drove home to a house full of flowers.

And I kept "hearing" from Angela. I felt this when I was meditating alone while our guests were snacking in the kitchen:

*Lighten up, people. I'm not actually dead, at least not what you liked most about me, i.e., what some of you called my spirit or my light. I'm wherever you are, and I'm not going any- where, unless you ask me to leave. And if you think this is weird, remember, I'm as natural as sunlight and birdsong.*

# CHAPTER 3

# The Weeks after Angela Was Declared Dead

On Easter Sunday, 2023, our house was filled with flowers, food, and overnight guests, including Angela's husband Charlie, Mananya, and Mananya's husband Stan.

During lunch, several of our guests expressed how Angela's passing had made them start to believe more in the possibility of life after death. Several of us — including me, of course — had felt what seemed to be Angela's presence. Our daughter was not at all religious, yet it seemed to me, and it had become apparent to several of our guests, that Angela was and is a powerful spiritual being who will be with us for as long as the universe allows.

I have felt her as a beautiful warmth and lightness in my heart, especially in our backyard (which Angela loved and helped us maintain), in our foyer (where we had set up a display of houseplants with Angela's encouragement and guidance), and in untamed tangles of green growth anywhere. Angela loved all plants, as did my father. She was a wildly successful and fiercely hardworking gardener, indoors and out.

ღ

As friends and family know, I often like to be alone. On Easter Sunday, 2023, everyone else went out for dinner while I stayed home. I was feeling guilty about not joining the dinner crowd, but I honestly felt emotionally drained and just wanted to lie down. As I stretched out on my favorite recliner, I felt Angela whisper:

*Daddy, go easy on yourself. Go easy on Mommy. Take one day at a time. Do not beat yourself up if you are not instantly back to normal. This could take months, or years.*
*Find joy in simple things. Write and do the gardening thing.*
*Mommy really needs you now. Don't fuck this up.*
*I love you more now than I ever did when I was in the body. Now I can love you from the inside.*
*Go walking by yourself. I will be with you.*
*Start throwing shit out. Clean the garage.*

Full disclosure: As of this writing, I still haven't cleaned the garage.

ღ

On April 12th, Mamie, Charlie, and one of Angela's best friends — Michelle Mèngshuâng Táng — flew to New York City to begin the sad task of gathering, consolidating, and distributing Angela's belongings from her apartment. Mamie was surprised to find Angela's apartment neatly organized, with the bed made. This was weird because Angela was famously messy and rarely, if ever, made her bed.

This is from Angela, dated April 13th:

*Daddy, in Buenos Aires I said that we need to earn the right to tell the truth by shoveling shit for a long time. That is not true on this side of things.*

*Ultimately, there is only one eternal truth in the universe, and that is pure love. AKA God.*

*Daddy, together let us campaign on to victory under the banner of pure love.*

*Daddy, you are a missionary. You were sent to teach about love. That is why you grew up with so much pain.*

*Be of good cheer. A much better time for you and Mommy is on the horizon. I am touching her heart and whispering there. You will see. She is beginning to understand better, and she's turning her heart to the light within herself, where I am waiting to hug her.*

On April 14th, Mamie flew back from New York City. In our backyard, the fuchsia and yellow ice plants that we had planted the year before were blooming magnificently, and the aroma of flowering bushes was intoxicating. When I went outside, I felt as if Angela was enjoying it with me.

But this was lost on Mamie, who is not a fan of gardens or the outdoors. When I told Mamie that I felt Angela was communicating with me, it was salt in her wounds.

In the days that followed her trip to New York City, Mamie sank into a deepening depression. At the breakfast table where we used to smile at each other and enjoy our wonderful good fortune, now she was tearful and grief-stricken, sometimes shaking, repeatedly saying that she was in so much pain that she didn't know how she could go on, and that she didn't really want to live much longer.

After comforting her as well as I could by listening, hugging, and holding her hand, I retreated to my "upper sanctum," the bonus room over our garage.

*Daddy, Mommy is in so much pain, it hurts everywhere. Give her space but be within reach and be patient. It will be worth it, I promise.*

I thought: "Mommy just said she doesn't want to stay in this world much longer. I find that very depressing."

*Daddy, don't blame yourself. Mommy is her own person. There is not much you can do except take care of yourself and be as kind toward Mommy as you can. And, for God's sake, meditate.*

Early on April 16th, I was meditating when I heard this:

*The answer is joy. Accept joy. Welcome joy. Allow joy to seep into every part of your world. It is at your spiritual core and all around you in everything all the time. It is pure love, the essence of the universe. And the way to joy is often through terrible sadness. So accept sadness as well. Embrace sadness as a mother holds a crying child. Joy will follow, in her own good time.*

As I wrote the above, I heard my wife close our bedroom slider. She told me she had just heard a baby crying and had gone outside to figure out where the sound was coming from. There was no baby crying outside.

On April 18th:

*We are all children of the spiritual universe, children of spirit, sparks from God's original fire. But as pure spirits, before incarnation, before human birth in the physical world, we are seeds only, not fully developed souls with full and complete dimensionality.*

*As humans, you are spiritual beings in physical bodies for a time. Those of you who develop spiritually can reach higher states of integration: souls grounded in dense physical matter while fully aware of the highest spiritual vibrations in the universe, of pure love, pure light, pure joy, and all-embracing wisdom and understanding. To achieve that, we must pass through the terrible and terrifying darkness of human life and emerge transformed into a real-life equivalent of Tolkien's Gandalf the White.*

*It seems ironic, but to become fully spiritual, we must fully experience the physical universe. The spiritual and the physical must grow together. They are NOT AT ODDS. Seed, soil, water, sun — and yes, the squalor and corruption that in gardening terms we lovingly refer to as compost.*

*This is our message, Daddy. WE ARE COSMIC GARDENERS. It's perfect. Your original intent, my "accidental" arrival as a "deus ex machina." Together, with Mommy, we shall be unstoppable. ♡♡♡*

*We shall loose the floodgates of pure love on this earth. And whatever evil shit they throw at us and the good people there, pure love shall triumph in the end, NO MATTER WHAT.*

*It's perfect, Daddy. This was meant to be. You, me, and MOMMY.*

*Daddy, allow the seed of pure love, pure spirit to grow and guide you for this important work that we need to do. We are all equal partners: You, Mommy, and me. She is the anchor. You are the sailboat's captain. I am the wind in the sails, urging you across the ocean of doubt and unknowing to the bright shore of total success and fulfillment of this brilliant destiny that the three of us share with the good people of planet Earth.*

3:05 PM (As I started meditating, joined by Mommy in another room):

*Dear Mommy,*
*I asked Daddy to send you this message, because I know you have not been able to feel me or hear me yourself. Yet.*

*We all know that you are incredibly effective at dealing with practical matters such as finances, cooking, working with contractors, and handling problems over the phone. However, Daddy seems to hear and feel me better at this time, partly because he's very sensitive and partly because he's been meditating and studying spiritual stuff all these years.*

*Honestly, meditation is probably the best way to develop a spiritual relationship with anyone, and since I'm now a purely spiritual being, meditation will help me connect with you. I see that you have started meditating with Daddy. Great! Please continue!*

*My endless love for the bravest person I know!*

*Angela*


I printed this out and shared it with Mamie. She was not impressed.

More and more, our backyard became my happy place. On April 20th, I felt Angela whisper:

*Cultivate joy in the garden of life.*


Meanwhile, sympathy cards, phone calls, text messages, and emails kept trickling in. Mamie and I were working to regain a sense of normalcy, while knowing full well that nothing would ever be the same.

Mamie said she felt like two people: on the outside, the usual Mamie who cooked wonderful food and managed our finances and took care of me, our house, and the feral cats who came to our back door; on the inside, Mamie felt completely devastated, always with sharp pain and heaviness in her heart. She said over and over that she didn't want to live much longer.

♡♡

Late in April we got a visit from Louisa Hager, who had worked with Angela in Weber Shandwick's Los Angeles office. Louisa shared this weird anecdote:

Angela and I had been working on a project together for months. It's a long story, but basically, to showcase how strong a new shampoo and conditioner made hair, we wanted to string an instrument with human hair. It wasn't working at all, despite many hours of hard work. One of our last conversations was about how nervous we both were that it would never work.

The morning after she died, the instrument-maker called our producer to tell him that the instrument was finally working and that it sounded beautiful. I started uncontrollably sobbing, because that is so classically Angela: to get right back to work, no matter what.

After Angela died, I wanted to check in on you both [John and Mamie], so I texted Mamie to ask when I should come over to the house. I left the chat, and when Mamie replied, telling me what time to come over, I reopened it to respond. But there was already a response typed in my chat box. It said, "This is your daughter. Come over." I think Angela had tried to text this to Mamie in early 2020, when Angela was with me and Mamie was coming to drop off her phone, but it was never sent. Especially since it wasn't there when I first texted, I felt like it was Angela telling us that she's still around — and that she wants us to be together.

From Louisa, and from many others with whom Angela had worked, we kept hearing stories of how Angela had touched their lives and careers in positive, often life-changing ways, and that she wanted passionately and worked tirelessly to make the world a better place, especially for women.

Being Angela's parents, we were intensely proud of our daughter, whom we thought we knew quite well. However, we kept learning that what we knew of Angela was only the tip of a massive iceberg.

♡♡

April 24, 2023
Approx. 1 AM:

*My purpose with you, Daddy, is to bring to wide public awareness the spiritual values of pure love, good faith, magnanimity, tolerance, and forgiveness.*

*These are values I tried to put into practice during my life, with obvious success. I want to share with the world the not-so-secret secrets that gave my life and career its pizazz. These are secrets that you, Daddy and Mommy, taught me by example and osmosis more than through lectures. They incorporate spiritual and common-sense principles such as the importance of investing in relationships through acts of kindness, and leading through love and inspiration, not by fear and intimidation. Some of these values are shared with Eastern cultures, although good faith is not a basic operating principle of the Chinese Communist Party (or many other governments and religions in the world, for that matter).*

*Daddy, with you I want to inspire a revolution of kindness, joy, and pure love.*

On April 25th:

*Humans need to be more chill. Ambition, aggression, bottomless greed, and rampant consumerism are destroying our planet's ecosystem and our future.*

*Daddy, this is a collaboration. It's not just you or me writing. It's us. And the future of our planet and the human race depends on us. All of us.*

*Whoever is not part of the solution is part of the problem. Unfortunately, too many people are part of the problem. We must do our best to change hearts, but ultimately, they are not our responsibility or our fault (although they can be our problem). We need to be at peace within ourselves about all of that.*

Around this time, another weird thing happened. Maybe the weirdest thing yet.

Every night, my wife and I leave our kitchen as clean as

possible. The sink is always spotless overnight. However, one morning I came into the kitchen and noticed an odd spot in the kitchen sink (see photo).

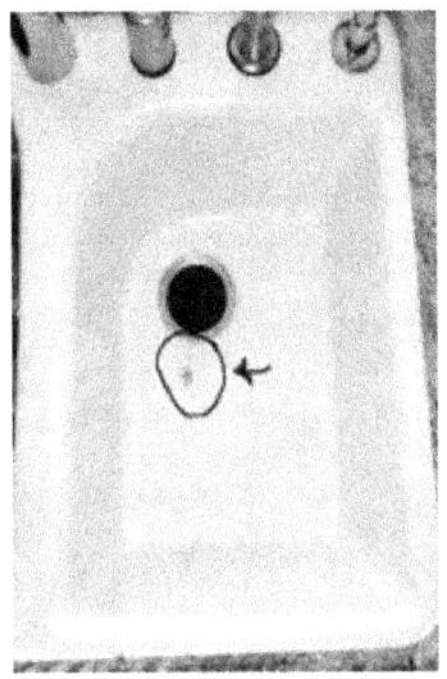

Looking at it more closely, I saw that the spot looked like a tiny tree. I took a photo of it with my smartphone camera and blew it up. Sure enough, it was a beautiful tree (see photo).

We can think of no logical or scientific explanation for this tiny tree that had appeared mysteriously in our otherwise spotless kitchen sink. Even if we had carelessly spilled a drop of something in the sink, why had it taken on such a beautiful form?

Angela loved nature in general, and trees in particular. Looking through Angela's scrapbooks, we saw dozens of small watercolor paintings, mainly of deciduous trees, like the one in the sink.

Our strong feeling was, and is, that our witchy daughter had somehow managed to materialize this lovely gift from the great beyond to show us that she is still with us, and capable of doing weird stuff to prove it.

Our grief continues to haunt us. But little signs like this have helped us greatly.


May 4th:

6:30 AM

Me (exhausted, with brain fog, and doubting everything): Oh, Angela


*Daddy, I am here. Listen. You don't have to do this. But if not you, who? And if not now, when?*


Me: I'm listening.


*Your world is hard. Very hard sometimes. It's heavy. Like training weights. To strengthen the soul. But ultimately, the lesson is to let go. Drop the weights, the heaviness. The weight of human life is all to learn, grow, develop soul strength. Not to carry forever. So let your heart be light. Don't buy into the illusion too deeply.*

*Pure joy is the ultimate reality. It comes from letting go of everything and embracing everyone.*

On May 5th, we received a card by US mail. It was from someone we had never met, a John DiMaggio in Fair Lawn, New Jersey. Inside the card was a long, handwritten note. With Mr. DiMaggio's permission, here is his note in its entirety. We greatly appreciate his words of comfort.

Dear Mr. and Mrs. Mears,

I wanted to write to you to express my deepest condolences on the loss of your daughter. I've been working with the ANDY awards for many years and was with them in Argentina. I know that this is an incredibly difficult time for you. My older brother passed away several years ago and my mother mourns him every day.

When Angela fell sick, she immediately had a lot of people by her side, caring for her. Gina Grillo was one of those people. I know that you've recently spent some time with Gina, so you know that above her work responsibilities, her most important job is being mother to her three sons. Gina ran to Angela and went into Mom mode. That maternal instinct took over and she spoke to Angela so gently and so lovingly. She did everything to make Angela comfortable while taking practical steps to make sure an ambulance was on the way and information to help the doctors was being gathered.

When we need support in life, it's human nature to want Mom. There's nothing else like that nurturing, loving support. Even though Angela didn't have her mom by her side, she had a mom by her side. I was moved to tears because I could hear the love, concern, and caring that Gina was giving to Angela and I deeply believe that it gave your daughter some peace. It may sound strange, but it was beautiful in a way to hear the motherly love surrounding Angela.

I know that there is nothing that can be said to make the pain go away, but I hope this can give you some comfort.

Yours truly,
John DiMaggio

As mentioned earlier, Gina Grillo is the President and CEO of the Advertising Club of New York, which hosted the ANDY Awards in Buenos Aires, Argentina this year. Clearly her behavior, which John DiMaggio described in this card, contradicted the clichéd caricatures of soulless corporate America and cold-hearted people in the advertising industry.

I feel compelled to again emphasize that my wife and I have encountered, over and over again, incredible kindness and magnanimity coming from people that Angela worked with, almost all of them in the corporate world of advertising, marketing, and PR. Further, even though my wife and I are of a politically liberal persuasion, as was our daughter, many of her close friends and coworkers lean more toward the Republican side of things.

The lesson for us is that loving kindness transcends political affiliation and broad stereotypes. If all of us can start to treat each other more like fellow human beings and even friends, and not as enemies from a different tribe, our world can be a much better place with a much better future.

As I was driving to work on May 5th at around 5 PM, a feeling came over me, a feeling of comfort and calm. It had rained, so I could see the mountains at the far end of the San Fernando Valley under gray clouds, with little flashes of sunlight peeking through. A jet was winging eastward under the clouds, and I thought, "That jet is going where it's supposed to go, taking people where they need to be." And it seemed, if only for an instant, that everything was perfect, that everything was as it should be, even though our daughter had died five weeks earlier.

On May 9th, we flew to New York City to attend the ANDYs Awards ceremony, which was held on the evening of May 10th. It was a gala event, kind of like the Oscars or the Golden Globe Awards, but for the advertising and marketing industry. It's an annual competition sponsored by the Advertising Club of New York.

During cocktails before the ceremony, I talked at length with a group of executives that included Tiffany Rolfe, who had sent us the long and touching message quoted above, about her experiences with Angela in Buenos Aires.

Our table was up front and near the podium where presenters announced the awards. Tiffany Rolfe was the first speaker at the podium. Choking back tears, she spoke about what had happened to Angela in Buenos Aires, describing Angela's work and personality in glowing terms. After a brief video memorializing Angela, Gina Grillo took the podium and announced "The Angela Mears Creative Star Mentorship Program," which would put twenty to thirty college graduates together with advertising industry leaders from the ANDYs organization to gain "tangible support to shine in their creative work environments."

After the ANDYs event, we were walking back to our hotel when something weird happened, reminding us of the "number 8" pattern we'd seen in Buenos Aires. Out of the blue, a homeless woman ran toward us from across the street, yelling: "Mr. Adams! Give me eighty-eight cents! I just need eighty-eight cents!"

Looking at each other, Mamie and I kept walking, but the woman followed us for more than a block, repeating: "Please! Just eighty-eight cents! Give me eighty-eight cents! I just need eighty-eight cents!"

Out of an abundance of caution, we didn't stop to find out why she wanted eighty-eight cents. I guess we'll never know.

In any case, the New York trip was a welcome distraction from what would be waiting for us when we got back home; for the worst was yet to come. We'll talk about that in the next book.

# Angela's Spirit

# Introduction to Part Two,
# by John

I have been meditating for more than fifty years. For at least twenty of those years, I have been writing down thoughts and feelings that come in moments of inspiration, often during meditation, but also at random moments, such as when I'm driving, hiking, watering the garden, etc. In those moments, I feel inspired by a mysterious inner sense.

People have asked me if I think I'm "channeling." I don't know. The word "channeling" creeps some people out. Including me.

To be clear, I never hear voices. Rather, I feel a gentle sense, a presence, almost a whisper inside me. It feels as if a better part of me is touching my consciousness in a caress of words and ideas. It's a lovely feeling of being connected to something much greater than my individuality.

On March 28, I began to feel a connection with Angela. It has continued ever since.

Naturally, many will be skeptical. "Hearing" from the departed could be a form of psychotic delusion. My mother, the psychiatrist, might have agreed with that explanation.

But some mental health professionals have started to see things differently.

In her doctoral dissertation at the University of North Texas (August 2011), psychology student Jenny Streit-Horn systematically reviewed thirty-five studies conducted on After-Death Communication (ADC). She wrote in conclusion: "Based on a thorough review of research, ADCs seem to be common, normal experiences with great potential for benefit."

Dr. Streit-Horn is now a clinical psychologist working in Texas.

In a 2022 issue of *Psychology Today*, Dr. Stephen Taylor, Ph.D., points to recent studies indicating that up to three-quarters of the bereaved report some kind of communication from a departed loved one.

Two therapists who specialize in traumatic loss and grief posted another article in the same periodical on March 15, 2024. Mark Shelvock and Jodi Gorham state: "Psychological research confirms that after-death communications are a normative and statistically common experience after a death-related loss. How people make sense of these experiences is incredibly diverse. These experiences are not representative of any underlying mental illness, abnormality, or psychopathology. Grief therapists frequently understand ADCs as a continuing bond, which demonstrates how we maintain relationships with the deceased and how grief truly has no prescribed timeline."

Also in *Psychology Today,* psychologist Jeff Tarrant, Ph.D., makes the point that feeling a connection with the deceased can help someone manage grief. He suggests that an approach to grief therapy called "continuing bonds" can greatly help reduce the distress of losing a loved one. He references a 1996 book, *Continuing Bonds,* edited by Dennis Klass et al., which introduces a new way of helping patients who have lost a loved one. Formerly, the dominant therapy model grief therapy was "breaking bonds" — saying goodbye at the gravesite and moving on. Klass and others offer an alternative model, "continuing bonds," in which the grieving are encouraged to maintain some form of relationship with their dearly departed.

A new form of psychotherapy called "induced after-death communication" (IADC) is now being practiced by hundreds of licensed mental health professionals around the world. Practitioners of IADC report that up to 75 percent of clients report "a deep sense of connection with the deceased loved one," and that sense of connection helps to reduce the intensity and the debilitating effects of grief.

That sense of connection has certainly been a comfort to me. I would even say that it has helped me heal from some of the profound feelings of loss that followed our daughter's death.

As I mentioned above, I felt the first after-death communication from Angela on March 28, 2023. I have "heard" from her almost every day since then. This book, however, only shares communications between March 28 and May 31, 2023. Future books will contain more. Much more. Because we seem to be just getting started.

Almost all these messages came to me during meditation, a time when I often feel very relaxed. I feel a joyful and very comfortable warmth in my heart. Of course, this could be my imagination. But I'll take it.

Regarding her "voice." More than hearing it, I experience it as a gentle sense, a glow of meaning to which I have assigned the words that you will see below.

Words. They can be problematic. I have tried in good faith to choose words that best express what I feel to be our daughter's intended messaging.

Angela was a passionate foodie. I present Part Two of this book much as Angela might have served a meal. The first section, called "The Angela Sutras," contains very short pieces that could be seen as appetizers. In later sections, some of the themes introduced briefly as "Sutras" are elaborated on in greater depth.

Over the years I have been inspired by many spiritual writings, including the Upanishads, the Bible, and the writings of Lao Tzu, Rumi, Hafez, William Blake, Ralph Waldo Emerson, and Khalil Gibran. In particular, I have been inspired by two recent series of spiritual books: *Emmanuel's Book* (by Pat Rodegast and Judith Stanton) and *Conversations with God* (by Neale Donald Walsch). I feel a personal debt of gratitude to all the people who gave us those books, and to the spiritual beings who seem to have inspired them.

The writings on the following pages — what I believe to be a collaboration with Angela and her spiritual team — inspire me. I hope they inspire you, too.

Thank you, Angela.

From Angela:

You're welcome, Daddy.

On March 27, 2023, a massive cerebral hemorrhage destroyed my brain and ended my human life. I entered a realm of indescribable beauty, wonder, and peace. It seemed to be composed of a lovely, gentle light that I like to call "pure love."

Since coming here, I have felt more and more that pure love is the basic stuff of this place, or dimension, where I am. We might as well call it "heaven." It also seems to me that pure love is the basic stuff of everything.

This collaboration between my father, my spiritual colleagues, and myself is just one small facet of a worldwide initiative by spiritual beings who are working with people of goodwill for a better world and a more loving, peaceful, and successful human race. We seek a bright future for everyone, in the spirit of pure love, forgiveness, and deeper, broader, higher understanding across multiple dimensions in every part of the world. Our work involves and affects every human being, and all beings everywhere.

# The Angela Sutras

March 28 to May 31, 2023

su·tra

/'so͞otrə/

*noun*

a rule, aphorism or brief passage of spiritual ideas
or philosophy

Whatever time it is,
it's always now
— which is the best time ever.

*Photo: A celebration of Angela's life with friends and family. October 14, 2023*

Pure love
is humankind's
secret sauce.
It's one of the main reasons
humans have survived so much horrible shit
for so many years.

A glow is only visible in darkness.
Love everyone and everything,
even those in darkness.
Even the darkness itself.

Cut everyone some slack,
including yourself.
Life in your world is hard.
Don't make it harder than it has to be.

Our choice:
A beautiful silence
to find calm, insight, and perspective
before bad things happen.
Or a terrible silence
after the shit hits the fan.

Let your heart be light.
It is the home of the light.

No matter how you feel,
you are pure spirit.
Safe and free forever.

Take time
away from the noise
and listen
to the whisper
in your heart.
That is where your eternal self resides.

Wear your responsibilities not like heavy weights but joyfully, like new clothing. Stop saying, "now I HAVE to..." Start telling yourself, "now I GET to...."

If we let it,
life can make us all
better people.

♡♡

A lighter touch in everything better suits our spiritual nature.

♡♡

Kindness is an art.
The most important
and the most beautiful art there is.

~ 59 ~

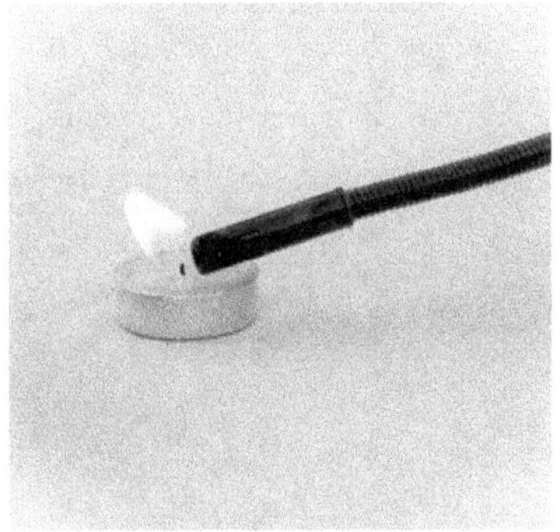

Every aspect of diversity serves a divine purpose.

God's pronouns are His/Her.

One day, one moment, one word at a time.

At your core is the pure light that shines in every galaxy.

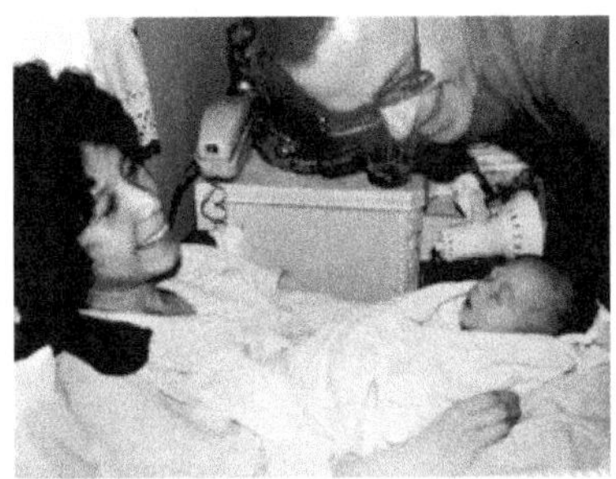

We all came into this world naked but not alone.

We were all conceived in lovemaking, by people who were probably naked, but definitely not alone.

When our bodies die, our souls enter a far more beautiful reality, naked again but never alone.

So why are people so obsessed with clothing?

Why are so many people afraid of being alone?

And by the way, why is anyone afraid of dying?

All opposites teach their opposite.

Irony is of the essence.

Stubbornness might serve
in the physical world,
but on this side,
it's a major obstacle.

When people say, "It's all good," that expression has
more truth than people can imagine. "All" means everything and everyone. Ultimately, everything and everyone is essentially good, because everything and

everyone are essentially expressions of pure love,
God's love, which — believe it or not — is very good.

The challenge here is to bring that spiritual essence of pure love and joy into our everyday lives. And given how things can go in your world, that's a considerable challenge.

Universal consciousness is peace.
Universal consciousness is joy.
Universal consciousness is pure love.
The door to universal consciousness is in every human
  heart.
The path to world peace runs through the heart of ev-
  ery individual human being.

The invisible is the source of the visible.
The spiritual is the source of the physical.
Spiritual life is the source of physical life.

Joy is of the spiritual world.
Misery is of the physical world.
To bring spirituality into the physical world
is to overcome misery with joy.

Joy and pleasure
are not the same thing.
Many physical pleasures can give temporary joy,
but ultimately lead to great misery.

Wisdom is choosing the path to joy.

Let your hearts be light,
and know that you are the light.
At the core of your being
is the same spiritual light
that created and permeates the universe.

In your heart,
you are pure spirit,
and free forever.
Remember that.

Don't make the mistake
of following others.
You are pure spirit,
proud and true.

Don't make the mistakes
of worry and fear.
You are pure spirit,
forever safe and eternal.

Take time away from the noise
and listen to the whisper in your heart.

# Conversations with Angela

## Where I am now

**Angela, all of us who knew you feel devastated by your death. Help us understand where you are and what it's like.**

First of all, I'm not dead. My body died, but so what?

Secondly, no words can really describe this reality. But here we go.

I am in a dimension of pure light, pure delight, among powerful beings of brilliant intelligence and love. No words can begin to describe any of this.

Everything is different here. We have bodies, but they aren't solid. We see and feel everything and everyone from the inside, because we are pure spirit, which is inside everyone and everything.

For many, pure spirit is a kind of mystery continent that few brave souls dare to explore. But they really should check it out, because it's great.

**Your mother is especially devastated. Since you left us, she has lost hope and belief in everything, and she feels disgusted with this world.**

Understandably. Your world can get pretty gross.

On this side, we are in awe of the courage required to live and continue living in the physical world. We are all rooting for your happiness, and everyone's, because joy radiates out and helps us all.

Human life is so important. The journey of human evolution and progress has only just begun.

**I feel you when I meditate, but that feeling goes away after awhile, and I wonder if any part of this conversation is real. Maybe I'm making all of this up. There seems to be a disconnect between spiritual experiences and my everyday human life.**

For millennia, there has been a disconnect between spiritual realms and the world you are in. That's why our work is so urgent, Daddy. We need to infuse spiritual consciousness into human life everywhere possible.

We are concerned about the rise in tensions around your planet. I say "your" planet instead of "our" planet, because, in the spiritual realms, we regard all life on all planets as sacred. We also enjoy visiting with beings on other planets. (For another book, perhaps.)

It might seem unbelievable to people who are suffering in your world, but the reality I am now experiencing is more real and more wonderful than anything in the physical universe. There is no pain here, only light and pure love. Infusing pure spirit, pure love into that material life, we can solve many problems that seem unsolvable. We can literally bring heaven to Earth.

**But we are hurting. It seems to require superhuman effort just to get through some days. It really is hard, especially for Mommy.**

I know. We know. Mommy is the bravest person I ever met, and the mere fact that she keeps going is awe-inspiring.

**She says she feels like two people: one person who is functioning normally, and another person who has lost all interest and joy in this life.**

Mommy is geared toward hard work and due diligence. She used to always say, "I'm going to try" with everything she was planning to do.

But here there is no trying.

Everything here is completely effortless. We realize that much of human life requires hard work, but where I am, there is no effort. Just by thinking, we can be anywhere in the universe.

On this side, there is no anger, only patience, forgiveness, understanding, and pure love.

On your side, people get frustrated by delays and obstacles. Dealing with those obstacles patiently and effectively is a valuable exercise for the soul.

Seen from our perspective, spontaneous acts of kindness propagate waves of pure love that we see as a beautiful light. Helping people sends ripples of joy throughout the universe.

At the risk of sounding glib, we in the spiritual world wish you in the physical world would lighten up and have more fun. Joy and lightness of heart are essential spiritual qualities.

Human beings have amusing concepts about the spiritual world. For example, when people depict angels, they often show wings. In reality, angels have no wings. We don't need them.

More importantly, while almost everything in the physical world requires effort, nothing in the spiritual world does. However, people bring effort to their spiritual practices, which is counterproductive, especially in some forms of meditation, such as Transcendental Meditation.

**Since your passing, Angela, a bunch of weird things have happened. For example, the image of a tree appeared mysteriously in our kitchen sink. Care to comment?**

What you call "miracles" are direct interventions where some of us in the spiritual dimension reach through the veil to shape events in the physical world for some urgent reason or purpose, often to get the attention of humans who would otherwise be unaware of our reality. In the great majority of cases, we prefer not to engage in these direct interventions, because it's like a teacher whispering answers to a puzzled student on an important test.

From a wider and more significant perspective, every human life is a miracle. So is the entire universe, when you think about it.

After my passing, my team and I have had a little fun planting little miracles around to get people's attention and offer physical evidence that any of this is real. It is real. Just like that little tree we mysteriously manifested in the right-hand side of your kitchen sink.

# The Purpose of This Book

My mother once told me, she used to call me "the little preacher," because when I was just learning to speak, I would stand on a step and babble with my arms open as if giving a sermon to a crowd. Through many phases of my life I have felt a weird calling, as if I was sent to Earth on a mission of some sort; but it  has never been entirely clear to me what that mission might be.

That feeling came back when I had the following exchange with Angela.

**Angela, on March 28, 2023, you seemed to say something like, "This was the plan all along." What exactly did you mean by that?**

Daddy, you have been preparing for this work fifty years or more. Developing skills in writing. Meditating every day. Listening to the whispers of your own heart. Reading stuff like *A Gift of Prophecy* and *Emmanuel's Book*. You've been channeling inspirational wisdom from the spiritual realms for dozens of years.

Meanwhile, I got famous in the world of advertising and marketing, then died and found myself in the company of beautiful, powerful spiritual beings, almost all of whom were once human beings themselves and who understand well the human condition and look upon the world today with great compassion and concern.

My career in public relations and marketing was perfect preparation for this: selling the human race on basic spiritual realities that can help everyone in your world and ours. You could say we're doing P.R. for heaven.

We want to help people on Earth make it safely through troubled and troubling times. We're focusing on pure love, because it is the most hopeful solution to the world's problems. It is unifying and unstoppable.

Pure love is also the basic stuff of the universe. It is the reason I was so successful, Daddy. I was raised in pure love by you and Mommy and Abu. Pure love is the heart of our message.

Our message is simple and clear. Like a dog's love. Pure love. Loyalty. To humankind. To human kindness. To planet Earth. To life on Earth.

Humans will have a better chance of surviving if they make pure love their priority. Dark times are almost certainly ahead, but the human race now has literally godlike power collectively. You must use it responsibly. Heroically, even. In the spirit of pure love. By far the greatest power in the universe.

It might get crazy-hard, but never despair. Pure love is the mother of all solutions.

Hope is pure love
projected forward.
Patience is pure love
taking its time.
Work is pure love
put in motion.

I want to emphasize that everything and everyone is essentially spiritual. Pure spirit is at the center of everything. Pure spirit is pure love. It is eternal. It is everything forever. Let's make it our priority. Always. The eternal over the temporary. It's not mumbo-jumbo. It's just common sense.

Time is growing short, Daddy. Very short. It's time for people to get serious about creating a hopeful future for life on Planet Earth.

Pure love calms people down. We need more calm in the world today.

Pure love is already present and flowing generously in and from billions of human hearts. Our job, Daddy, is getting humankind back to the business of saving itself from itself and saving the world from human madness and stupidity.

Humankind needs to get down
to actual human kindness
and pure love.
It is by far the greatest power.
It is the essence.
It is of the essence.
It is the essential stuff of the universe.
It is the power behind all creation.
It is all pervading, the heart and soul of the universe.
It is the ultimate solution for ALL our problems.

Pure love is the only way to a better future.

Humans need to be more chill. Ambition, aggression, and rampant consumerism are destroying your planet's ecosystem and your future.

The future of your planet and the human race depends on us. All of us.

We must do our best to change hearts, but ultimately, others are not our responsibility or our fault — although they can be our problem. We need to be at peace within ourselves about all of that.

All life is an interaction of the spiritual universe with the physical.

Nothing would exist without the spiritual.

Everything is animated by spiritual energy and intelligence.

We need to bring more spiritual values into human life.

Not just in families or circles of friends, but in communities, nations, and the whole world.

Planet Earth is a garden of souls. Daddy, we who love gardening and the human race can do much to cultivate this garden to encourage people around the world to embrace pure love and greater understanding.

Let's cultivate joy in the garden of life.

Earth's people are at a pivotal point, and horrendous catastrophes are increasingly probable. We must do all we can to make the best of a bad situation. And the secret sauce for that is pure love.

♡♡

Many people are, or seem to be, beyond help. The best we can do is whisper a seed of pure love and understanding, then let them be. The seeds of pure love will grow in good time, regardless.

♡♡

Our mission is to reach people who might not be otherwise reachable with the message and the healing, enlightening power of divine love, pure love. Many are ready. The time is now.

However, many are NOT ready to accept even the idea of pure love, so we need to be patient and have faith in what we know to be true.

♡♡

Many good people
have given up.
They need whispers of hope,
of pure love and freedom,
of the real possibility of a better world.

We want to help humans and spiritual beings work together more closely in the future. We can develop a civilization guided and dominated more by pure love and wisdom, less by greed and lust for power. Less cruelty and more human kindness.

We know, we know. It's been tried before. Now we'll try a slightly different approach.

Volcanoes, geysers of light, are rising from human hearts around the world. A rebirth of pure love is well underway. We who write this book are only a small part of this massive spiritual renewal that is encircling your beloved home planet. May all humans embrace the best within themselves, the pure love inside them that will save them all, spiritually as well as physically.

The heartbreaking cries of humankind have moved spiritual

beings in the higher realms to reach down more directly in the urgency of this moment. We ask that people everywhere partner with us for the survival of all life on planet Earth.

Deep inside every human heart is a spark of divine love and wisdom. We encourage all of you to embrace and grow that spark, for the good of all.

The time is short and the road ahead might be long and rough, for the darkness in human hearts can be hard and stubborn.

Dominated by rage, greed, rigidity, and fear of the un-known, many will cling to the ways of the past. Much mayhem and destruction is already happening and much more could be unavoidable. People of goodwill and kindness must work together to survive. Together, we can build a new and better human civilization in the ashes of the old.

In human form, Daddy, I was a team builder and a team leader. I learned and now I'm teaching the importance of teamwork. The human race can be a team. It should be a team. It must be a team. To work together for its own survival.

# Pure Love

**Angela, you mention "pure love" over and over again, but in many parts of the world, hate seems to be getting more prevalent.**

Which is why we need this book, this work, this campaign.

Pure love embraces everyone and everything. It extends into the darkness. It fills the darkness.

The darkness wants love. It needs love. Pure love pours itself into the darkness with endless love, so the darkness is also permeated by pure love, which is total and unconditional. It is the essence of everything and everyone. It just needs to be recognized, emphasized, and brought out in people.

Pure love is the source of humankind and human kindness.

It heals and saves everyone it touches, which — believe it or not — is everyone.

It is the inner essence of everything and everyone.

Pure love purifies.

It soothes.

It comforts.

It protects.

It is our divine mother.

Keep going back to the source: God's pure love, the ultimate source of everything and everyone in the universe. That source is also inside you, in the center of your heart. When people say, "Listen to your heart," the real meaning is: "Listen to God." In the core of every heart, God waits with infinite patience.

You are always welcome in that temple inside yourself.

♡♡

Pure love is humankind's secret sauce. As a matter of fact, it's the secret sauce of the universe.

♡♡

Pure love inspires beauty.
Beauty inspires pure love.

See the beauty.
Feel the beauty.
Record the beauty.
Increase the beauty.

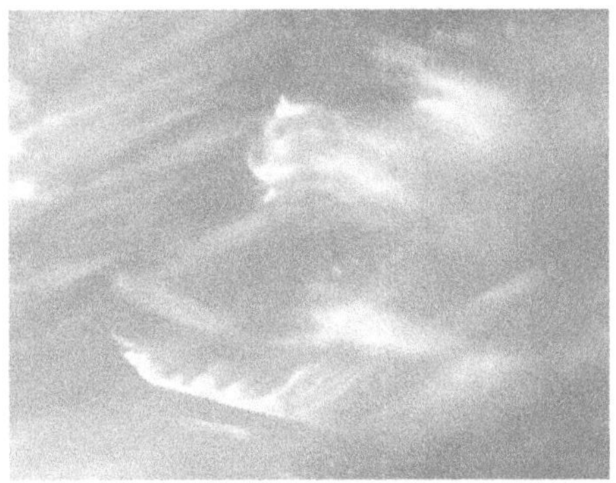

A bright new day is waiting for the human race when more people embrace pure love.

Pure love is win-win. It's baffling that everyone is not already making it their first priority. It's pure joy. It's peace. It's unlimited prosperity. It's the end of war and misery. Why, oh why are we even having this conversation?

Some people might find the idea of pure love too sweet for their taste. But pure love is beyond any particular flavor, and it's got zero calories!

Maybe pure love seems boring because it has no car

chases, gunfire, or explosions. Maybe it makes some people nervous because it doesn't have the official seal of approval from their favorite religion. Or maybe it sounds too liberal because of what it could mean: justice, empathy, and kindness; healing the sick and helping the poor; patience and forgiveness; tolerance and acceptance of differences.

I will never get tired of saying this:
I am pure joy.
I am pure love.
We all are.
But in their bodies, people forget.
I am here to remind them.
And you.
Especially you, dear reader.

Sending pure love into the universe benefits everyone, especially the "senders." The ripples magnify in their return, until it becomes a brilliant lovefest of epic proportions. We send out waves of pure love, and they come back as tsunamis.

Pure love dances with the darkness
and transforms it into joy.
Pure love is our essence.
Allow it to express itself in you.
It's one with God and the universe forever.
That means we are all safe.

No act of kindness is futile. It sends ripples of joy throughout the universe.

But it's a different matter if that act of kindness is calculated, with an expectation of reward or reciprocity.

In spontaneous acts of kindness, forgiveness, and generosity, pure love flows from the divine spark at the heart's core and into the entire universe. The thrills of joy extend into the great and mysterious beyond, from which they return, greatly magnified.

Relax and feel the light of God's love, deep inside your heart.

Regardless of whatever impatience, restlessness, or frustration you might feel, there is divine perfection in everything at every moment.

Most importantly, in you, dear reader.

**Is pure love the same thing as what they call true love?**

Yes. Pure love includes personal love that is selfless, deathless, and unconditional. It goes beyond anything that anyone can understand.

**Does pure love continue after death?**

Once we have truly loved someone, we will always love them, and vice versa.

Not just in this life, but in past and future lifetimes as well.

Every connection of pure love creates an invisible bond that stretches between the people who love one another, whether those people are still in physical bodies or not.

These bonds also connect loving people with other living things: animals, plants, and all forms of life, visible and invisible.

Seen from our perspective, these bonds look like beautiful threads of sunlight piercing through dust and darkness.

Since so many have loved so many others, the network of loving connections has become infinitely intertwined and overlapping, like a giant ball of luminous yarn.

To the spiritual eye, Earth has become a glowing orb of divine love.

On the spiritual level, Earth's radiance is unimaginably beautiful.

The brilliant threads of pure love extend beyond Earth to all beings throughout the universe, so that in the dimension where I am, the entire creation appears as a vast, self-luminous network of divine beauty and pure love.

Of course, to the physical eye, it looks different.

Firstly, physical love — even what they call "true love" — can get complicated by jealousy, rivalry, control issues, possessiveness, and rage.

Some people even think of love as being the problem. To the contrary, pure love is the solution to practically all problems faced by the people of Earth.

The main problem is the domination of human behavior by uncontrolled physical impulses, tribal instincts, and self-centered emotionalism; by rage, greed, hatred, bigotry, jealousy, obsession, and pettiness. Since religions are institutions created by human beings, these tendencies infect most religions. However, within all religions are countless sincere lovers of life, God, Buddha, and/or humankind. Pure love cares nothing about nationality, religion, race, sexual orientation, or group membership. It is universal and without condition or limitation.

Pure love needs humankind's full attention if the human race is to survive current tensions and hostilities between nuclear powers.

This planet and its dominant race — humans — are worth saving. We in the spiritual realms are committed to doing everything possible to work with people of goodwill to save planet Earth from human beings, and human beings from themselves and each other.

♡♡

May pure love awaken every heart
from killing and cruelty.
May pure love stir every heart
for peace and healing.
May pure love open every heart
to deeper understanding.
May wisdom save planet Earth
from mindless greed and exploitation.
May wisdom save planet Earth
from human hatred, rage, and foolishness.
May wisdom save the human race
from its own destruction.

# Freedom

**What is the relationship between pure love and freedom?**

It's a direct relationship.
Pure love and freedom go together.
Freedom is a natural consequence of pure love.
It is an expression of pure love.

**But in the news these days, there seems to be a lot of nastiness and fear, and in certain countries, many are ruled by harsh governments that severely limit personal freedoms.**

Planet Earth is a free will zone. Human beings are not to be deprived of their personal freedom, as long as they are not harming themselves or others.

In the spiritual realms, we hesitate to intervene directly in human affairs. We give people the freedom to make their own choices. As much as possible, humans will be wise to do the same.

This is win-win. First, it empowers others to choose for themselves and learn from those choices. Second, it frees people from the illusion that they are responsible for other people's choices, and it allows everyone to focus on their own choices on their own path.

We respect every individual, and as much as possible, within reason, give them freedom to work things out within their own sacred space. People and systems that deny that freedom violate the laws of the universe. If anything could fairly be called evil, it is that violation of individual freedom.

**But what can people do? Under authoritarian governments, working for greater freedom can get you killed.**

Remember that the death of a human body is not the worst thing that can happen. Believe me, I know.

The human race will prosper to the extent that people can let go of fear and smallness of spirit to move your world into a more hopeful future.

**I can hear people saying, "Come on, really? You seriously expect human beings to let go of fear and smallness of spirit? What you suggest is impossible."**

Impossible?

Much that people take for granted now once seemed impossible. What seems impossible now will one day soon be commonplace.

The human race has achieved so much. Social and technological progress have accelerated with breathtaking speed. But now you face your biggest challenge ever: evolving spiritually in time to save yourselves and your world from your own destructive impulses.

World superpowers sometimes act like toddlers with loaded handguns pointed at each other. But instead of handguns, they have nuclear bombs and missiles that can turn your entire planet into a charred wasteland.

We can think of ourselves, Daddy, as loving parents who coax their children to put down those guns and get back to more useful undertakings.

Come on, people. We can do this.

# Meditation

Note from John: This section of the book would not exist without the quiet mind and the open heart that have blessed me during more than fifty years of Transcendental Meditation, as taught by Maharishi Mahesh Yogi. Practically every word in Part B of this book came to mind when I was meditating, or at least relaxed. I invite you, dear reader, to explore the peaceful realms of pure spirit within yourself. I believe you'll find it to be time well spent.

Note from Angela:

I never learned meditation, but now I kind of wish I had. Where I am now, meditation seems like the best thing a person can do when they're in a human body. Members of my team here know more about it than I do. I just know that meditation can take a person to levels far beyond the understanding or experience of most of us here. Full disclosure: much of the material in this section comes from others here who know far more about meditation than I do.

Our purpose is to bring more spirituality and pure love into human life. Meditation is a perfect way to do just that.

**But a lot of people find it hard to meditate. They're too busy, too agitated, too preoccupied.**

It takes self-control and self-discipline to meditate every day. However, when you exercise self-control and self-discipline, you take command of the parts of the universe pertaining to you. Which happens to be much more than you can imagine. This spiritual development will benefit you endlessly as you go through this life and future lives, as well.

**You say meditation requires self-control. That requires effort, doesn't it?**

Getting into a meditation routine — even getting oneself to sit down and meditate — requires effort and discipline, but while meditating, people need to give up all trying, all effort and expectation, as well as self-doubt and self-sabotage. Have faith in your highest Self, which is one with God and impelling you to victory, even as we speak.

**Don't we have to give up a lot to meditate?**

Giving up certain things can be instrumental in finding spiritual peace and progress. As much as possible, minimize drugs, alcohol, gossip, and the company of toxic people, for starters.
Let go and fall into the arms of the Divine.

**But to some, it seems kind of selfish to go off alone and leave people wondering WTF you are up to?**

Meditation is the most socially responsible thing you can do. It might seem antisocial when you go away from other people and close the door, but meditation can connect you to the higher consciousness within yourself and everyone else. It paves the way for a more peaceful world and human race. It can get you beyond the pettiness of the ego and limiting thoughts and feelings.

Meditation cultivates pure consciousness, which grows inside people like a seedling of pure love that spreads throughout the human experience. Cultivating that seedling can take many forms. There are as many ways as there are people. Because spiritual growth is natural, every human being is already growing spiritually in his or her own way. Spiritual growth can feel scary sometimes. However, on the spiritual side, there is always progress and evolution, because the soul remembers every lesson and grows irreversibly.

Pure joy is the ultimate reality.
It comes from letting go
of everything
and connecting
with everyone.

I am spending time in silence.
You should, too.
Our choice: a beautiful silence
before bad things happen,
or a terrible silence
afterwards.

Let your heart be light.
It is the home of the light.

Agitation is not good motivation.
Let it pass.

Peevishness is not at all helpful.
Let it pass.

Anxiety is toxic.
Let it pass.

**Some people seem to be completely devoid of any interest in spirituality.**

Most people are consumed by everyday pressures, concerns, and distractions. We can't blame them for that.

But even though few people seem to realize this, every person has a divine spark, which is like the seed of a new universe. For most, that seed is dormant. In its own time, the seed will sprout and grow.

**I have friends and family members who have learned meditation, but stopped. If meditation is so great, why do they stop?**

For meditation to work, one needs to abandon all ego effort and preconceptions. Relaxed, open, and effortless. But in adapting to the pressures of life in the physical world, people's minds are focused on effort and critical thinking. Effort and critical thinking work down there, but not up here, and not in meditation.

In meditation, a person can let go of everything basically.

Beyond grasping and grabbing, we can experience oneness with the universe. Believe us, that's a great feeling.

**I have had a taste of that in meditation myself. I wonder, though, if people who haven't had those experiences can relate to the material in this book.**

Words and phrases from the depths of consciousness can take people in that direction when they are ready.

Greet every new day with joy. Meditation makes that easier.

Every new day is an opportunity to experience and express the divine. I don't mean the divine like a stuffy, churchy thing, but rather as a beautiful, joyful, vibrant, even sexy thing.

**What about hatha yoga?**

We also strongly recommend yoga before and/or after meditation.

Open your arms and reach them up to the sun, to the sky. Stretch in the open air. Stretch your body and unkink your nerve fibers to let the pure love energy of the universe flow through you, as it has always wanted to do.

Feel your deep insides.

A lighter touch in everything better suits our spiritual nature.

**But Mommy and I have felt this terrible heaviness since you passed.**

We know. We hope these communications from our dimensions will help to lift that heaviness.

Let your hearts be light, even in your dark and heavy world. The darkness and heaviness accentuate the light and the lightness of heart.

# Grief

**What can we say to comfort people who are dying?**

Where you are going soon is a place of indescribable beauty and peace. There you will feel no pain, only boundless love and joy. Some dear souls you loved will be there to greet you. All fears and worries will be gone. You will find yourself in an ocean of pure love, joy, peace, and light.

**What can we say to comfort those who are losing or have lost a loved one?**

Know that you and your dear one are losing only their physical body — which, let's face it, can get pretty disgusting, especially with illness and old age. Where they are going is so beautiful that there are no words. Be at peace, even in all your pain, knowing that they will be greeted with love by others you love who have passed, and it will be a reunion far happier than any family reunion they have ever attended.

The sublime joy
of the spirit
can ease our grief.

Death of a dear one
can rouse us
from our spiritual sleep.
Or it can shock us
into a deeper, darker sleep
of bitterness and blame.

We make what we want
out of everything.
Let us make the best
of everything.
EVERYTHING.

Know that we who have left physical embodiment
have not left you,
but wait at your shoulder, or in your heart.

It's actually our joy
to comfort you,
to inspire you,
our dearest ones.

Beyond all the grief in your world,
endless joy is waiting.
For you.

On a dark canvas,
the painter needs light-colored paint.
On a light canvas,
the painter needs darker and more colorful paint.
The spiritual is light.
Matter is dark.
Together, they make artwork
that we call the universe.
God is the ultimate artist,
and we are all God's apprentices.

**Whether or not that's true, here we are, Mommy and me. We are both devastated. Mommy especially.**

The only certainties of the physical world are suffering and death, with the possibility of temporary joys and pleasures.

The certainties of the spiritual world are boundless joy, pure love, and eternal life.

That's why meditation is so important. It's a doorway to the spiritual world inside you and around you. To pure love and healing. To healing from grief and all kinds of trauma.

# General Advice

As you, dear reader, can surely understand, our daughter's passing plunged us into a deep and terrible sadness. Mamie especially. Both of us need to hear this section. I think we all do.

In particular, this section shows our daughter's love of gardening. She was a fabulously successful and ambitious indoor gardener, and the Chicago apartment she shared with her husband Charlie was a de facto greenhouse.

Our daughter was also fascinated by squalor and loved talking about poop. You might get a sense of that here.

Let things be your fun, your joy.
When things go wrong, see the humor and the irony.
When things go right, celebrate!
When horrible shit happens,
remember the First Law of Composting:
The nastier the shit,
the greener it will make plants grow
in a year or two.

Very little progress happens in a straight line.
Trust the detours and setbacks,
even defeats in important struggles.
You can reach your goals
if you keep the faith and try new ways.
Trust God, the universe, and your own divine spark.

A glow is only visible in darkness.
Love everyone and everything, even the darkness.
Cut everyone some slack, including yourself.
Everyone is doing the best they know how.

That includes you, dear reader.

**How can we love everyone? Especially people who have been cruel, abusive, or treacherous? I don't want to love them. I want to kill them.**

When we develop a relationship of trust and understanding with the universe, we feel less compelled to settle scores or seek revenge and vindication. Universal justice, the laws of karma, are a reality, although not always visible or apparent.

We don't love people for their sake. We love everyone for our own sake, because in pure love there is joy, healing, and safety.

**Angela, when you were in your physical body, you used to complain about lazy people, including me. Now you seem to have switched gears majorly. Your message seems to be, "Stop trying. Just love everybody."**

We're not advocating for laziness, but for evolving your attitudes. Remember that everything is what you make of it. A hard job gets harder when people are always complaining. With a light heart, you can carry a heavier load.

Wear your responsibilities not like heavy weights but joyfully, like new clothing. Change "now I HAVE to..." to "now I GET to...."

♡♡

If you let it, life
can make you all better people.
If you keep your hearts and minds open —
if you stay alert and pay attention —
you can learn valuable lessons
from just about everything.
And everyone.

Anything that sharpens your perception
and deepens your understanding,
your feelings and your appreciation
is priceless.

People tend to obsess, to see things from a narrow perspective. You naturally tend to fixate on the physical perspective, because you are in physical bodies focused on physical survival and physical sensations. However, frustrations with physical limitations and traumatic experiences such as death shake people out of a purely physical orientation and encourage them to seek a higher understanding.

No matter what, people are always learning spiritual lessons and growing in their own unique way.

In meditation, people can dive into their own spiritual interiors and gain insights that will greatly help their growth and learning. They can also experience more pure love, which is very healing.

In the spiritual world, which you can enter through meditation, no effort is necessary. Here, there is no thought of trying.

We simply let our divine nature
be what it is:
pure love,
vibrating and expressing itself
in an infinite variety of forms and realities.

**Sometimes I hate myself and doubt this work and everything else. So does Mommy. We're both wrestling with horrible feelings. Mommy keeps saying she wishes she had spent more time with you, given you better advice. She wishes she had been a better mom.**

Stop beating yourself up.

Just stop.

Because in your heart is the same divine light that made the stars.

**Are you saying we are God?**

In essence, yes, but not in terms of God's power or God's personality. In you is a spark of God's original light. That means you and God essentially have the same spiritual essence. Accept that. Embrace your own portion of divinity. That part of you can be your best friend, your best mentor, your spiritual GPS.

Allow God's love and light to express itself in everything you do.

Let your own divine nature — pure love — come out of hiding.

Let your own divinity heal and restore the entirety of your being: physically, mentally, emotionally, spiritually.

**That sounds great, but how can people feel God's pure light when they're struggling with bill payments, unruly children, nasty neighbors, and bad decisions?**

God's pure light is always inside everyone. People just need to take a moment to feel that light inside them. Especially before making important decisions.

In the pressure and craziness of the physical world, people often make choices that bring unwanted consequences. They feel like losers. But every so-called failure, every disappointment, every setback can pave your way to humility, which is key to spiritual growth and progress.

**Sometimes the struggles of life seem endless.**

Maybe it will help you to know that pure love, pure joy, is always waiting inside you. For that reason, we can never be where love is not.

The reality is that we are always held in the loving arms of our divine Mother.

# The Future

**Can you see the future? What is coming that we need to know about?**

No one can predict the future, because so much depends on the choices of so many people.

However, as you know, new technologies are accelerating like crazy, while spiritual progress and wisdom seem to be lagging behind. That is a recipe for disaster. Dark times are on Earth's horizon.

However, in darkness, people are more open to the light. A much better world could result from the catastrophes that have already started. Just as demolition often comes before construction, widespread devastation could pave the way for a brilliant future.

The oceans are rising and the world's climate is changing. These changes will force massive relocations and refugee crises. The international tensions already rising due to overpopulation and climate change could at any moment spiral into global thermonuclear war. On our side, we are doing all we can to prevent this. But people can be stubborn in their craziness.

As people rebuild cities and civilization after the devastation that now seems inevitable, the human race must realize that, long-term, planet Earth cannot sustain, nor can the human spirit long tolerate, the following:

Greed
Racism
Bigotry
Sexism
Tribalism
Oppression
Fossil fuel consumption
Warmongering
Ideologies (religious or political) based on hate and fear
Extreme disparities in wealth

None of the above can end well.

But please, people.
Do not worry.
Rise above fear.
Let's do our best
to bring the light of pure love to the world
as quickly, widely, and inclusively as possible.

Time is growing short.
Urgency is growing.

A viable future for your world depends on people working together, not tearing each other apart. Class struggle has not been very successful because it has often operated on the basis of hatred and violent conflict. What is needed is reasoned dialogue and mutually respectful exchanges between and among people of different classes, religions, and other "tribes," so that there can be mutual benefit and not mutually assured destruction. It comes back to a change in consciousness: a change in people's hearts, minds, and spirits.

Anything to save the world.

Everything to save the world.

Hey, everybody! Let's see what we can do to save the world!

# Madness

**I have often wondered if I have lost my mind, listening to mysterious "whispers" and putting them in a book. What's your perspective on mental illness?**

You are not crazy, Daddy. The communication we are sharing is real. Remember that Induced After-Death Communication is actually a form of therapy. I hope our communications have helped you.

**They have. But Mommy is still hurting bad.**

I know. We know. It will take time for her to recover.

**She keeps saying she will never recover.**

She will never be the same. But who will?
But back to your question about mental illness. From our perspective, much of the human race has gone mad. Humans are destroying their homes. People are mindlessly poisoning

Earth's water, air, and soil, which are the sources of their biological survival and well-being. Where I am, on the spiritual side of
the veil, this is not a big problem, because we spiritual beings
exist without biological means of support; but on your side, the
physical human side, it is a very real threat to the continued ex-
istence of all life on Earth.

People are using fossil fuels, promoting nationalistic bellig-
erence and religious intolerance, breeding indiscriminately,
and blindly buying products and consuming unhealthy foods
whose production do great harm to Earth's ecosystem.

Let's be very clear about this. If human beings continue on
their current path, life on planet Earth will soon be rendered
far more difficult and unpleasant than it already is. Humans
might soon be able to live on Earth only with respirators and
HAZMAT suits allowing people to breathe toxic air and live in
a highly radioactive environment. This is clearly unacceptable.
The fact that so much of humanity is blithely rushing into such
dire outcomes seems to us in spiritual realms to be the very
definition of madness.

Those who like to call themselves "pro-life" would be wise
to look at our current situation from a broader and more scientific perspective. Is it really "pro-life" to be polluting planet
Earth, the source of your biological life? Many drive gaso-
line-guzzling trucks and cars, pouring tons of pollutants into
the air. Many keep guns stored at home unsafely, often allowing children to kill themselves or each other. Many resist all
efforts to control gun violence. Yet many have spent decades
and millions of dollars to ban abortions, calling themselves
"pro-life." It seems crazy to force children to be born into a

world where they will suffer greatly before they are shot to death by another crazy person in another school.

**Of course, many of those to whom you are referring call themselves Christian. What would you say if you were to speak directly to them?**

I would say that Jesus was and is a wonderful teacher, healer, and spiritual leader. But he was not and is not the only wonderful teacher, healer, and spiritual leader. He performed miracles, but he was not and is not the only one who can perform miracles. He was and is a child of God, but he was not and is not the only son of God. We are all God's children.

Didn't Jesus say words to the effect that we will do greater things than he? So let's get started! And the best place to start is by seeking the kingdom of God within ourselves. That's actually the first thing everybody should be doing, if they can. Secondly, people would be wiser and better followers of Jesus if they expressed pure love in every way possible. Finally, everyone — no matter what their

religion or non-religion, or their spiritual beliefs or non-be-
lief – everyone would be wise to refrain from judging, co-
ercing, or manipulating anyone else in a spiritual context.
Everyone has his or her own soul, spirit, mind, and personality. They all need to make their own choices and be at
peace within themselves.

# PART THREE

# Longer Talks from Team Angela

Especially in this section, Angela seems to be working with a team of spiritual beings who are sharing information and advice almost like university professors. Therefore, the material here is presented in a kind of lecture format.

Angela has indicated that she is serving as a kind of conduit for messages from higher realms and that she herself cannot yet understand all of this material.

# The Big Picture

The news is not just what is happening around you. The most important news is what is happening inside you.

As a member of the human race, you are part of a grand experiment to see how divine intelligence works when injected into a sophisticated biped organism whose mechanical operations are more or less controlled by a complex biocomputer. That biocomputer makes choices, generally with only a dim recollection — or no memory at all — of the spiritual being that was inserted into its heart at birth. That spiritual being is always there, watching and often whispering secrets and guidance. The wisest are those who prioritize listening to that spiritual being, which is the essence of what we all are and the reason we all are here.  It is not really a separate part of you humans, because it is integrated into your biochemical life system. However, at birth it becomes in most cases secondary in awareness to the biological, physical realities in which you find yourselves.

Looking for pleasure and approval, people spend lifetimes

going down paths that often lead to misery and pain. By paying attention to the divine light in their own hearts, people can experience more joy, more peace, more success. And by "success", we are not talking about money, fame, and power. We mean finding solutions to life's challenges, especially one's own, in personal terms. Personal satisfaction and happiness might not be glamorous, but in the end they're all that really matter.

In your world, there are many for whom success means victory in combat. For them, victory means killing all their enemies. But in spiritual terms, violence and killing are unwise, and can trap the soul in lifetimes of regret. The "cycle of violence" is an unfortunate reality that is now, with the possibility of nuclear war, no longer acceptable.

The pure light of God's love in your heart is your greatest treasure, whether you feel it or not — and you can feel it more by meditating.

Meditation is the best thing you or just about anyone can do, because it unites the conscious mind with the transcendent super-consciousness that is at the heart of the universe. It is a way to personally experience the universal reality, the oneness or unity that connects everything. It connects you with your own divine intelligence.

Not everyone can perceivably benefit from meditating, for a variety of reasons, but everyone in the world can benefit from people around the world meditating. This is why meditation must be a priority, especially in the days to come.

Humankind is a screaming child held to the breast of our divine Mother, the goddess of pure love whom many humans do not seem to care about or understand. Comfort, healing, understanding, and peace are waiting for us all when people relax and trust the universe and the best within themselves. Meditation is a wonderful way to do that.

Lasting peace can be found only in pure spirit. The good news is that people can experience pure spirit without dying. However, to truly experience pure spirit, people must leave their egos at the door, along with everything related to the ego: effort, expectation, preconceptions, pride, self-congratulation, and self-deprecation. The joy of pure spirit is countless times more wonderful than anything that can be achieved through ego-based thoughts or actions.

Most people, like me (Angela), had to die to experience this. But the good news is that people don't have to die to experience spiritual realities, especially if they meditate.

Pure spirit, pure love — the basic stuff of the spiritual world and everything — is inside and around everybody, all the time. It pervades everything.

Think of a high-rise building. You can be on the first floor, and somebody else can be on a higher floor above you and you would never know it. You're at the same address, and Google Maps would show you together, but you can't see each other. The spiritual world has many "floors," many vibrational frequencies. At the "top" of the building, the "penthouse," is where the administrative center is, the "Holiest of Holies," the Controller of the Universe, the Divine Mother, and the Almighty Father. Beyond or above that, there is no vibration. That is the Transcendent, Brahman.

Many people are on the first floor, or even the parking

garage under the building. They're "there," but their knowledge and experience of the building is limited, and so is their point of view, which is street-level or lower. In time, especially with spiritual disciplines such as meditation, people rise to higher levels, and their view changes.

Drugs can give a temporary glimpse of higher levels, but some drugs — especially when done excessively — can damage the nervous system and make longer-lasting experience of higher states of consciousness next to impossible.

The wisest and safest approach is by regular, consistent practice of spiritual disciplines such as yoga, meditation, selfless service, and sincere, heartfelt prayer. These and other spiritual disciplines gradually and sustainably raise the level of consciousness by exercising and training the human nervous system to experience higher vibrations and dimensions on a daily basis. This isn't glamorous or sensational, but it's the best way forward for the human race. It requires patience, persistence, perseverance, self-control, and — hardest of all for very smart, good-looking, ambitious people (like I was as a human being) — HUMILITY.

# The Physical World and Duality

Everything in the physical universe is based on duality, the coexistence and interaction of opposites. In pure love, there is no duality. The unifying power of pure love holds the universe together. All of it.

Everything in the physical world, and in creation, is process. Nothing in the universe is final. Nothing. And nothing in the universe is absolute. Nothing. Including where I am, in the spiritual realms. Every aspect of the manifested universe is relativity, duality. Only the absolute unity beyond all this is absolute, yet it pervades and permeates all this. The non-vibrating essence of pure love pervades and permeates all that is.

All thoughts are vibrations. Pure love is beyond duality, beyond thought, beyone vibrations.

Everything in the universe of duality can be seen as a double-edged sword. Nothing is entirely good or entirely bad, even according to human definitions.

Everything is hybrid. Nothing is purely this or that. There is in the universe nothing that is totally good or totally bad.

Therefore, walk in joy, on two feet. Walk in the light, even surrounded by darkness. In darkness, the light has greater beauty and meaning. In darkness, people hunger for the light.

Don't take anything too seriously. On a certain level, nothing matters and nothing IS matter.

Everything and everyone serves a purpose in the great universal order.

The physical world can be so attractive, so difficult, and so filled with problems and dangers. Dangers have always been there on your planet. But increasingly, human beings are the main source of Earth's problems and dangers. Humankind is creating disasters that threaten the survival of all life on Earth. People need to think soberly and responsibly about what kind of future they want to create.

The human race has developed godlike power, to create and to destroy. Humans need to think more deeply and responsibly about their impact in their world. They need to be more proactive. They need clearer heads and bigger hearts. They need to open their eyes and see the danger signs and take preventive measures.

Everything is temporary, and on a certain level nothing matters. But surely, people want their children and grandchildren to grow up in a world that has not been devastated by monstrous human behavior.

The physical world is both sticky and shaky.

Here's the sticky part: Matter can be glamorous, attractive, and sensational, drawing you in and holding your attention. Earth's gravity holds people in place so they can do their thing here on your planet. Many earthly attractions, especially food and sex, can be addictive. So can drugs and — the most addictive drug of all — power. So people get stuck in your sticky world.

However, earthquakes shake things up and remind you that everything there is temporary. The same thing with other natural catastrophes such as fires, floods, and droughts, as well as man-made catastrophes such as wars and the destruction of nature.

Everything that has been created can also be destroyed. That includes the human body — which is, after all, a THING. It only becomes a person at birth, or very soon before birth. Death of the body (because its spiritual essence, its soul, has left) also shakes people up, again reminding everyone of the transitory, temporary nature of human life and the need to look and think beyond the physical.

So the physical universe sucks us in and spits us out, or — to be gross about it (which never bothered me, as those who knew me well can attest) — the physical world eats us up and poops us out.

However, here is the fascinating twist. In the statement above, the "poop" — the part of us that survives being "eaten" — is the part of us that the physical universe cannot digest or destroy: the soul. Our spiritual essence. That in us that will never die. Our ultimate, imperishable reality. Our light that shines on in the darkest night. The spark in our hearts that is forever, has always been, and will forever be one with God. The most brilliant, adorable, wonderful part of us, which most of us spend our lives trying to ignore at our peril, as humans.

Many dismiss their most essential truth as an annoying, whiny voice in the back of their heads. In truth, people would all be wise to listen carefully to their conscience, which counsels them to kindness, mercy, forgiveness, honesty, and humility.

Instead, people often listen to, prioritize, and identify with the following:

Their petty egos

Their bodies (which can easily get sick, injured, or horribly mangled, and will all, without exception, die)

Their possessions (which can be stolen or destroyed in a heartbeat)

Their families and friends (who can abuse them, oppress them, or betray them)

Their sensory pleasures (which can cause a wide range of problems if overindulged in)

Their drugs (which invariably have side effects and are often addictive and fatal if overused)

Their accomplishments (which are often quickly forgotten)

People struggle in vain to create permanence in an impermanent world, castles of sand before rising tides.

Science can see beyond our limited sensory perceptions. Science tells us that matter, which appears solid, is in fact mostly empty space. The illusion of solidity is created by molecular bonds and atomic interactions. The lesson is that, ultimately, bonds are the supreme reality of the physical universe. And it's especially true for humans. Our relationships, our connections and interactions, define us. And the bonds of love between us, the spiritual connections, are — more than anything — the reason the human race on planet Earth is worth saving.

# Speaking of Religion

According to many religions, especially in the Western world, a masculine God, AKA the Almighty Father, is the supreme authority in the universe. However, without our Divine Mother, His power is meaningless and empty. Therefore, HIS/HER is the deeper truth of God, beyond gender distinctions.

People have been brainwashed to think they are not spiritual beings with godlike potential. But they are.

Some religions have taught people to believe that they are fallen creatures like Smeagol in the Lord of the Rings trilogy, doomed to hell unless they seek rescue from whatever religion. That is also not true.

Many religions have done a lot of good. Some of them have also done a lot of damage. Regardless of your religious beliefs, or your hostility to religion or spirituality in general, I'm here to whisper a message of pure love, pure joy, peace, and freedom.

Practically every religion arose from pure love. Unfortunately, pure love does not seem to be a high priority for some modern-day religions.

I died young so that I could bring the world this message from heaven: pure love can save your planet, your people, and your ecosystems. This is not a new message. In fact, it's at the heart of practically every religion in the world. Still, this message hasn't reached a lot of people. And lately it's gotten incredibly urgent.

I was not a disciple of Jesus per se, but I am a disciple of pure love, which was at the heart of Jesus's message. It also happens to be at the heart of everything and everyone.

The answer is not in any one religion. The answer is in the source of all religions: the light of pure love in every heart.

Jesus talked about gaining the world but losing your soul. This is very deep wisdom. However, it seems to have contributed to a split between the spiritual and the physical, the "worldly" and the "holy." This split has become enmity in many cases. It has put spirituality out of reach for "worldly" people. It has also contributed to conflict, wars, and even genocide in the name of religion.

What we want to do here, Daddy, is to enrich your world, even save it, by infusing it with pure love, the energy of heaven. We are promoting spiritual values based upon God's pure love for everyone and everything, and inside everyone and everything.

# PART FOUR

# Angela's Wish List

For me all life is a miraculous gift. The death of Angela's body — while devastating us emotionally — also brought unexpected blessings.

In one unusually long session, Angela communicated the following:

Since I am not actually dead, Daddy, I ask that people talk about me not in the past tense, but in the present tense.

I also wish:

That everyone who loved me shall live like they mean it.
That people shall love the ones they love like they mean it.
That people shall show up for the ones they love and be totally present for them.

That everyone shall work to save Earth like they mean it.

That everyone shall work to save the human race like they mean it.

That everyone who does not intentionally threaten or hurt others shall be safe and respected, loved and protected.

That every child shall feel heard and held, because they are being heard and held.

That no human being who is not wanted shall be born.

That no human being shall be forced into sex or into giving birth to an unwanted child.

That sex shall be an expression of loving and being loved.

That sex shall be a joy for all parties who participate, and that none of the parties shall be forced to participate, or manipulated into participating.

That the word "tender" not refer only to steaks, but also to how we treat every living thing and our planet.

That the word "life" refer not only to biological phenomena, but to spiritual beings as well.

That every human being shall think, speak, and act with the utmost kindness and conscientiousness.

That every human being shall honor the divine spark within their hearts in every moment, for all their lives.

That every human being shall treat others, and be treated, as is appropriate for those who have the divine spark within their hearts.

That, henceforth, divinity shall be known for pure love and joy, and not for cruelty or judgment.

That religion shall teach pure love and not fear.

That spirituality shall focus on joy and liberation, not oppression.

That love of God shall bring joy in freedom.

That the human spirit shall feel more winged and less chained.

That human beings will walk and talk with angels and God while still in human form.

That human beings shall obey the sweet suggestions of their hearts.

That peace will be our future, and that war will exist only in history books.

That the unique good in every human being shall be recognized, encouraged, and developed.

That all who disagree shall do so in peace and with reason.

That mutually respectful dialogue, reasoned arguments, and demonstrable facts, not violence, shall settle all disagreements.

That service to humankind shall be honored as service to God.

That those who work for peace shall be honored as much as those who fought bravely in war.

That those who threaten human life shall be respectfully prevented from causing harm, injury, or death.

That those who pollute our water shall be given polluted water to drink.

That those who pollute our air shall be given polluted air to breathe.

That those who violate our trust shall lose the freedom to violate anything.

That religions shall teach kindness and not blind faith.

That cruel people shall be deprived of their ability to inflict their cruelty on others.

That yoga and meditation shall be available, facilitated, taught, and encouraged throughout the world.

That love and respect for all human beings — regardless of race, gender, religion, ethnicity, nationality, or sexual preference — be taught in every home and every school.

That pure love and freedom of choice shall be the golden banners for the human race.

# Thoughts About Angela's Wish List

Dear reader,

Someone asked me if I felt drained or exhausted after transcribing "Angela's Wish List." It was, after all, a rather long session.

The answer is: No, I didn't feel at all drained. In fact, I felt inspired, refreshed, and renewed. Almost all the after-death communications from Angela occurred during Transcendental Meditation, a completely effortless technique that can also leave you feeling inspired, refreshed, and renewed.

I wonder if maybe Angela's spirit is interacting with my nervous system while I'm in a receptive mental state. Maybe Angela is not whispering to me so much as she is activating and inspiring a part of my own brain, or a part of me that is wiser, calmer, happier, more insightful, more hopeful for the future of the world. I truly don't know. I only know that I feel grateful for this experience, for the opportunity to know a better version of me and of our daughter.

# Afterword

I feel losing our daughter has made me a better person. Just as earthquake damage can motivate people to remodel their houses, making them better houses, Angela's physical death has motivated me to change my attitudes and lifestyle in what I feel are positive directions. I have more hope for the future of our world and the human race. The loss of our daughter in this world has forced me to open my heart and mind to the mysteries of the Great Beyond, and to trust the universe in new ways. It has given me faith. Not religion. Faith. Assurance. The deep assurance that life does not end when our biological hearts stop beating, or arteries burst in our veins and drown our brains in blood. A feeling that pure love pervades the universe and waits silently in the heart of everyone and everything.

The devastation of our daughter's death, the crater she left when she died, has opened my heart to my wife, the person in the world most traumatized by this loss. Mamie and I had drifted apart. We had different schedules. I usually went to bed hours after her, and we rarely ate breakfast together. But the gaping hole in our lives is a wound that I feel we are beginning to close and heal with our love and respect for one another.

Our daughter's body is gone. Her ashes have been scattered in California, Chicago, and Pennsylvania. Our lives have been shattered forever. But deep, deep down, I feel it's far from a complete loss. Her spirit — her wise, brilliant soul of pure love and healing — has touched and continues to touch many lives, as we have heard from countless people who loved her. Her spirit continues to touch and deeply comfort me from the inside. It nudges me lovingly to finish work I had abandoned, to fulfill the promise of my birth and the purposes of my life. It has ripped apart the veil separating heaven and earth in my heart and allowed angels to connect with my own insides. Where there was mystery, now there is clarity: inside every human being is a seed of divinity, with a potential destiny far beyond our imagining. We can and we should realize and fulfill in physical reality the best that we can envision, and perhaps even more.

We are all part of something that is far greater and more magnificent than ourselves and far beyond our wildest imagination. We are all part of a team of beings throughout the universe working together — whether we know it not, whether we believe it or not — for a transcendent purpose, the fulfillment of creation.

Life cannot help but break us; but it does so to force us to grow into a greater wholeness. The shell, the husk of every seed must break for the seed to fulfill its purpose. Every grain must be ground to powder for us to have bread and pasta. The cracked pavement must be torn up for us to have a smooth road with new macadam.

All our madness feeds a greater sanity and wisdom. Destruction and decay feed future growth.

Have no fear, humankind. The dark clouds on the horizon are thunderheads bringing the rain we need for the future of our world.

Shakespeare wrote, "Sweet are the uses of adversity." Sweet, indeed, is the spirit of courage and hope within us that can help us heal and create a better world than we have ever seen.

# Appendix:
# Remembrances of Angela

I'm in shock and still trying to process everything. Angela was my best friend, and a part of my life through every difficulty and success we both had since we were 12. The impact she had on me will resonate forever.

**From Kurt Bitter,**
Classmate at Chaminade College Preparatory

I had the overwhelming pleasure of being Angela's newspaper advisor at Chaminade. One of my fondest memories — and there are so many — is of Angela during her junior year. We needed a Sports Editor. No one wanted the job. I asked Angela not because she'd ever written a sports story or had a particular passion for sports-oriented anything, but because I was certain she could do just about anything. Of course she said "yes" in the very calm, confident way I think she might have been born with. Fast forward a month and we practically had to turn down students who wanted to be sports writers. Naturally. Because [of] Angela. I'm certain there are so many people who have stories with a similar theme: Just because [of] Angela. Prayers and thoughts and all love to you, Mamie, and all who she loved and who loved her back.

**From Stacy Kruse,**
Angela's newspaper advisor at Chaminade

Angela was one of the wisest and wittiest students I've had the joy of teaching in my 30-year career. Her intellectual curiosity about literature and life and her deep insight into the written word and the world beyond it made me a better teacher. I realized early in the school year from Angela's writing that there would be little for me to teach her about that skill — I simply needed to give her good reasons to write and then get out of her way. Angela was great fun to know and her laughter kindled joy in those around her. Losing Angela from this world hurts beyond measure. She belongs to the ages and the stars now. How lucky we were to live when she did and to know her.

This afternoon Brother Tom came into my office, saying "Our Angela? Our Angela?"

I sent a prayer request to the community today when I heard the heartbreaking news of Angela's passing. BT is no longer our principal but is still on campus, working as the academic and social counselor for our international students, all of whom are from China. He is, as you can imagine, beloved by them. And he is, as you can imagine, fiercely protective of them, so many thousands of miles from their home. He is, as ever, one of my closest friends and mentors.

BT said today, tears in his eyes, "Angela was one of the very best students in my career — THE BEST, let's be honest. How she'd come into my office when she was the Talon editor, fighting for her stories. And that voice. And that writing. My God! Her writing! Do you remember her Valedictorian speech? She was just a force of nature. She could have run this place, even then, even as a senior. My God, such a beautiful human being."

**From Jennifer Alison Poole,**
Angela's English teacher

Angela truly was unlike any person I've ever met. Her wisdom, introspection, and intelligence made her an incredible writer and philosopher. Her warmth, openness, protectiveness, and kindness made her one of the best friends I've ever known. Based on the outpouring of grief and love over the last week, I know I'm not alone in this sentiment.... On top of everything else, Angela was an amazing mentor and teacher who was compelled to share herself with the world through brilliant writing and good food. On this aspect, I'm particularly indebted. While she and I first bonded over a humble bowl of Kraft macaroni in our freshman dorm, she was also the person who first introduced me to the most amazing food I've ever eaten, including but not limited to, sushi, cilantro, oysters, shellfish-in-general, hot pot, quick-pickled onions, medium-rare steak, pork buns, and soufflé. While I'm grateful that I can revisit her recipes on "The Spinning Plate," it's truly the incredible insight and unparalleled emotional intelligence of her writing there that has made her blog so difficult, but also nourishing to tearfully revisit over the last week. Angela understood humanity and what it meant to live in a way that few people do.

Thank you, John, for being so communicative on Facebook. I can't imagine how difficult it must be, but it is so appreciated. I don't know what else to say but to send you and Mamie my love.

**From Alan Fast**
Classmate at Northwestern University

If you have a remembrance about Angela that you would like to share, please feel free to email me at john@angelasbook.com.

John Mears lives with his wife Mamie in the Los Angeles area. He has taught English to adult immigrants for more than forty years. Interacting with thousands of adults from around the world has given him joy, inspiration, and hope for the human race.

John's daily meditations have cultivated a feeling of connection with everyone—especially with his daughter in the afterlife.

www.ingramcontent.com/pod-product-compliance
Lightning Source LLC
Chambersburg PA
CBHW071317150726
47997CB00002B/503